Thinking of
Miller Place

Thinking of Miller Place

A Memoir of Summer Comfort

Ethel Lee-Miller

To Beatriz
Enjoy Miller Place
Ethel Lee-Miller

iUniverse, Inc.
New York Lincoln Shanghai

Thinking of Miller Place
A Memoir of Summer Comfort

Copyright © 2007 by Ethel Lee-Miller

iUniverse books may be ordered through booksellers or by contacting:

iUniverse
2021 Pine Lake Road, Suite 100
Lincoln, NE 68512
www.iuniverse.com
1-800-Authors (1-800-288-4677)

Because of the dynamic nature of the Internet, any Web addresses or links contained in this book may have changed since publication and may no longer be valid.

The views expressed in this work are solely those of the author and do not necessarily reflect the views of the publisher, and the publisher hereby disclaims any responsibility for them.

ISBN: 978-0-595-43877-8 (pbk)
ISBN: 978-0-595-69128-9 (cloth)
ISBN: 978-0-595-88200-7 (ebk)

Printed in the United States of America

Contents

Acknowledgments

My husband, Hank Miller—For saying in your matter-of-fact way, "Of course. Write this book."

My Finn, Eileen Erickson—For your steadfast support and love in this and all my endeavors.

My sister, Ingrid Bruens—For always providing the protection of being the older sister.

My parents, Gladys and Allan Erickson—For bringing appreciation of art, education, and dance into my life, and for simply being.

The Boonton Scriveners Writing Group—For those rich Mondays of being together in the presence of dedicated writers and supporters.

The Write Group of Montclair, and the Memoir and Muffins Group—For countless opportunities to share chapters in progress.

My Family—There would be no memories, no retelling, and no book if we hadn't spent those summers in Miller Place.

William Paterson University Toastmasters of Wayne, New Jersey—For opportunities to share storytelling.

Carl Selinger for spreadsheet organization; Grace DelaFortiere for French vocabulary; Mary Garland, writing partner and muse; every second grader I was privileged to teach at Washington School, West Caldwell, New Jersey; The International Women's Writing Guild, which sustains the belief that each of us has a story worth sharing; Troop 1624 Girl Scouts of New Jersey; the Barnes & Noble of West Paterson, New Jersey; Panera Bread of West Caldwell, New Jersey; and Borders Books and Music at the Wayne Towne Center, Wayne, New Jersey, for encouraging the combination of laptops, coffee, and bagels.

Introduction

How can the name of a place evoke such an overall and shared feeling of comfort? Those two words, "Miller Place," do just that in my family. Miller Place was the security blanket my sisters and I covered ourselves with when bad dreams, disappointments, and feelings of insecurity threatened to overrun the spontaneous joy of childhood. For two months each summer our family retraced the route to that sleepy country town on the northeastern end of Long Island, an almost magical oasis of freedom and exploration.

There are rough edges in every childhood. Miller Place offered us an idyllic timeout from feeling the scrapes from our rough edges. Miller Place had its pokes and holes, but the serenity and security we felt there allowed us to look at the pokes and holes without falling through. I know it allowed me space to step back and see what was real—as if sitting on the cushion of a soft and comfortable couch.

These are my memories of a special time and place in my childhood. My parents, twin sister, and my older sister, even the neighbors, may have slightly different or even hugely skewed views.

For anyone who has had an intimate friendship, relationship, or sibling connection, sifting through personal recollections and opinions is seasoned with that other person's input—solicited or not. Only a twin can imagine the blending that happens between twins.

My twinship influenced how I saw, felt, and remembered everything—often as part of a duet. For my entire childhood, the years of this book, I had no interest in anything—walking, running, laughing, whispering, or holding hands—unless it was with my twin sister. Any separate activity or thought was entertained only if there were a connection to my twin or could be shared later with her. For the first twelve years of our lives we were like a single cell, only beginning the process of dividing into two separate beings.

I could have expressed more of my mother's jagged edges with her father in this memoir, or the issues of trying to raise three girls in the 1950s when being a *good* mother and housewife was rigidly defined. I have deliberately set the boundaries of my story to reside within the innocent awareness of a preadolescent girl—a twin often shielded from harsh realities by the fact of being a twin and never being alone.

As a family systems counselor I've viewed the amazed looks on the faces of adult siblings as they talk about their mom or dad. Siblings they may be, but their childhood history is like that of separate families. Ask any adult about a childhood incident, and if there were four siblings, you'll get four different stories. My sisters and I have had such differing views of episodes.

As an adult, I've dealt with my own issues of finding self-worth, defining function and dysfunction, and crafting my own beliefs and values from the foundation of those of my parents. I have chosen to examine and present Miller Place as the backdrop for those beliefs. Yet, this geographical place is strong enough to almost be its own character. Miller Place knew the summers of my childhood at their best, with only a few contrasting flaws to keep joy in the foreground in comparison.

The image of a red ribbon is a symbol of the freedom I felt in Miller Place. The Miller Place white house with black trim and red shutters remains in memory as my landmark of safety.

My practice of using Miller Place memories as a comfort is still a way of connecting with my sisters. "Remember when …?" often leads to "Really? I don't remember it that way!" But the smiles and comfort are always there for the three of us. My memories have overflowed my mental files and spilled into oral stories for friends and then onto paper.

Why write about such a place? There's no high drama, no intrigue, no edginess. Perhaps that is exactly why I have felt the need to write about Miller Place. It is meant to be a book that is a balm, a bedside comfort at the end of a day when the energy and willingness to tackle another family challenge is depleted.

The names of my relatives have remained the same; other characters' names have been changed. The essence of personalities remains intact. The dialogue is meant to enhance the mood and perspective of this particular reading experience. Take this book and spend time with it as you would sitting with a friendly storyteller.

Thinking of Miller Place is the result of shaking the snow globe of my lifetime of memories, letting the flakes of old black-and-white photographs, and shared memories settle to show a view of that small world of my childhood. Some chapters turned into writing straight from family stories. Some emerged only after the retelling of facts laid a foundation for the richness of memories. Insertions, then deletions, were followed by sitting with a piece until just the right phrases spilled out.

Chapter One:

My Red-Ribbon Place

Grandma brushed the little girl's hair back and up into that one-fisted hold in preparation for a skinny, silky ponytail. She twisted the rubber band around the bunch—one, two, three times. Then pulled the tail up and out to the sides to tighten the hold. The little girl felt some hair pull, but only a little. She pushed the bangs over to the side.

"Wait, turn around." Grandma's hands deftly tied a thin red ribbon into a bow around the ponytail. "There. You look sweet. Now skedaddle."

The little girl skedaddled. Off Grandma's lap, out through the screen door, down the wooden steps, across the burnt grass of summer, and up the slight hill of the driveway. The dust from the sandy driveway felt cool and soft on her bare feet. A soft phfft sound as the ball of her foot hit the dust. The air smelled faintly of the crabapples from the tree up the hill.

She ran past Grandpa's flower gardens, past the cement birdbath, past the old stone fireplace. It felt as if her six-year-old body was lifted entirely off the ground. The red ribbon lifted up in the running breeze. The little girl was fast, light, and pretty.

◆　　　◆　　　◆

This red-ribbon scene is a memory from my childhood over half a century ago. I remember not only how everything looked but also the smells and the sounds. I use this memory as my foundation for self-comfort, my calming vision of "It is all right."

I believe each of us has, from childhood, a magical place and a beckoning to an almost spiritual terrain. For some, that place may represent years of unconditional love and acceptance.

1

It may be evoked by a folded and refolded picture, like the Breck Girl ad torn from a magazine that my twin sister kept for years as a totem of the beauty that would someday be hers.

It may be an overheard remark carelessly dropped in the air. "Yeah, she's got that family artistic talent too."

It may be a red ribbon tied with love.

The self-centeredness of childhood is always with us. I was fortunate to be granted a time and place when this self-centeredness faded to the background, and I learned some lessons—some of them disturbing, some fearful, some about prejudice, some of loss. Some of these lessons were gloriously exhilarating, like a crush, a glimpse of beauty, or a feeling of peace. My special place gave me the gift of childhood summers of being blessedly unaware, while I could get my feathers fluffed out like a newborn bird.

There are earthquakes under this magical terrain. That's not what I'm talking about. I'm talking about the foundation for my true inner self. It was during my Miller Place summers that I got to know this inner me, who is free, at peace, and as smooth and placid as the Long Island Sound at sunset.

That peaceful, free me has become layered over through the years with every-day mistakes, the clumsy loving of parents, the raw curiosity of childhood, the pricking of adolescent self-consciousness, and the shadows and bursts of maturity, but my red-ribbon experience has sustained me. I have been blessed with the dynamic memory of the enchanted place where this occurred.

In my memory, I am resting in a hammock between a childhood that was and the reality of today. In it, I am in a place where I can still, if only in my day-dreams, take off my shoes and run barefoot up the hill.

If you don't have a red-ribbon experience or your own red-ribbon place, I offer you mine—in a sleepy New York town of the 1950s called Miller Place.

◆   ◆   ◆

"School's out! Saturday we go to Miller Place!"

How many times did my sisters and I chorus this opening cheer to summer? We spent every summer in Miller Place. Although I loved the beginning of school each September, by February I was looking through the calendar pictures of March, April, and May to get to June again. June and Miller Place. My mother had been going to this same place, her mother and father's summer house on the North Shore of Long Island, since she was a girl.

Each time we traveled to Miller Place it was an all-day affair. Our journey began from our suburban town in the middle of Long Island, that 110-mile long island that many people locate by simply asking, "Isn't it part of New York somewhere?" If you went west from our town, you went through increasingly more crowded towns into the counties of Queens and Brooklyn, until you crossed over the Triborough Bridge into Manhattan in New York City—that faraway fashion and culture center that included the Museum of Natural History, the United Nations, the Statue of Liberty, and my most dreamed about city place, Radio City Music Hall. Radio City was home of the world famous Rockettes. If I had a choice as to what place to visit in New York City, I knew what would be the best—watching those Rockettes in colorful, spangled outfits do their incredible ten, twenty, thirty high kicks in one long, practiced, precision line.

Nevertheless, if you were lucky, like we were, you went east on Long Island. Then it was a far different journey—Sunrise Highway East to the Northern State Parkway, then to Veterans Highway. The eastward trip took you through increasingly less-populated towns, until the roads shrunk to single lanes. Towns were villages of one or two buildings—a store, maybe a library, small clapboard houses, and corn stalks that waved from farm fields along the way. East was the way to Miller Place, to our summer oasis by the beaches of the Long Island Sound.

Grab that taped carton for the car and ride with us.

The Erickson Family—(front) Ethel and Eileen, (middle) Ingrid,
(back) Gladys and Allan

Chapter Two:

On Our Way!

It was the first Saturday of summer vacation. We had been up since just after sunrise, and our old station wagon was stuffed with summer supplies.

"You'll never see out the back window," my mother cautioned.

My dad winked at me. "It's fine. It's fine. This way the twins can ride in the back."

My father, mother, and older sister, Ingrid, were in the front seat. Dad drove with Ingrid in the middle and Mom in the co-pilot spot. My twin sister, Eileen, and I always rode way in the back. "The back" in a station wagon was not the back seat. It was the way back by the rear window. The rear seat was technically for passengers (sometimes Ingrid was the passenger), but for my twin and me it was the physical division between grown-ups—the powerful ones—and two little wiggly six-year-old twins.

That glorious Saturday morning the rear seat was piled high with cartons of clothes, food, and one box for our paper cutout dolls and dolls we had chosen especially to take to Miller Place. Our identical Ginny dolls, small plastic dolls about eight inches tall with sticky vinyl hair, had been the special dolls for several summers. The only difference in our dolls was the hair color. Mine had blond hair; Eileen's had brown. Their carefully packed little-girl clothes were in their original cardboard box, along with our square chiffon scarves, which we pretended were queenly ball gowns draped around their pudgy bodies. *What fun was it to play dolls if they weren't movie stars or princesses?*

Our places in the car were fixed. Dad always drove, but my mother held the map. Sometimes Ingrid sat in between them. It seemed to me that my sister Ingrid had always been an adult-in-training. Her arrival in the world four years before us gave her power to boss us around. She paid for this power by being excluded from the fun we had in the back. Since the station wagon had bench seats, and our travels predated the era of seat belts, staying seated was enforced by my father's, "Down in the back, please."

Now this could be interpreted as "sit" or "lay down." Riding way in the back, Eileen and I really could lay down with our heads behind the rear seat, feet up on the rear window, which we thought was hysterical. I liked to wave to people in cars and figured this idea was easily reciprocated. How funny to wave to some kids in the back of their car, and at the next glance only see four bare feet stuck up against the window.

"Sing," came the command from our driver.

This was part of the trip that was well known by my sisters and me.

"You are my sunshine, my only sunshine."

After years of singing together, my sisters and I seemed to be able to start on the same pitch.

"You make me happy, when skies are gray."

"You'll never know, dear, how much I looooove you."

Giggles.

"Please, don't take my sunshine away."

Even today, just one line of that song can fill the atmosphere with a sense of belonging. I have no hesitation in singing it in the supermarket or at the mall. Just start humming.

Driving to Miller Place, the conversation was a running commentary of the trip. Ingrid, Eileen, and I took turns marking the miles with anecdotal recitations. There was a sense of security in our world by the repetition of the Miller Place journey. There was something very satisfying about knowing this was how it would be, no surprises, on the way to Miller Place.

"There's the sign for Port Jefferson," I chirped. Onto Route 25A. "There it is, the green sign for Port Jefferson. When will we go to Gramma's for sundaes?" Sure enough, the front seat map holder and decision maker answered, "No, we want to get to the house first." It was more of that security surrounding Miller Place.

Past the harbor town of Port Jefferson, we wound down the narrow curved road into the little village of Mt. Sinai, where we got a glimpse around the bend of the salty Long Island Sound.

We stopped at the Davis Peach Farm with its small front-yard wooden stand tended by an old, old woman we thought was Mrs. Davis.

"Think she's still alive?" one of us always asked as our station wagon's tires made that crunching noise on the gravel driveway.

"Yep, here she comes." It could have been any old lady who tended the stand, but because she came out of the Davis house, we automatically figured that was Old Mrs. Davis.

The stooped woman moved at a tortoise pace down her porch stairs to the wooden baskets lined up on the table. Sometimes she didn't come out. Then we took a large basket of peaches and put the money in a metal pail with a black hand-painted sign—PAY HERE.

I was curious about Mrs. Davis, not so much because she was old but because she was a member of the Davis family. The Davises had been in Miller Place forever; I heard they were really, really rich and yet here was old Mrs. Davis selling peaches.

Didn't make sense. Maybe it was a hobby for her old age.

Years later, when I worked at the local department store as a salesgirl as a second job to pay the debt of early adulthood overspending, I pretended I was a Davis.

"I don't really have to do this job; I'm just doing it for fun like my Aunt Davis."

When we got the peaches in their scratchy wooden basket, the first thing I did was put my nose down close to breathe in the sweetness: the perfect scent of summer. Then, I rubbed my fingers back and forth over the peach fuzz till it rubbed off like lint and the skin was really smooth. When I bit into it, the juice ran down my chin, and the tangy taste was cool and soft.

We went around a bend in the road along the inlet. "Oh, there's the church! Oooh, it looks so nice."

And it did, all white, from the top of the steeple to the front double doors.

"Mom, will we go to church tomorrow?"

"Yes, of course."

Just after the church was the curve in the road past the long low Wagon Wheel Restaurant—Bar & Grill.

"Your mother worked there when she was a teenager." My dad offered this information casually with a knowing smile at my mother.

"Oooh." I looked at my mother, trying without success to imagine her as a teenager. Was she pretty? Did she flirt with the customers? She worked at a bar? She didn't like it when Daddy drank, doing all she could to keep hard liquor away from him, and sighing whenever he reached for a new can of Rheingold beer.

In an unusual burst of conversation, my mother spoke. Even though she directed her words out the window as if she were speaking to the Wagon Wheel, she had to know we'd hear her even way in the back.

"Back then it was called Captain Roman's Inn. I was a waitress during the summers in high school. When the restaurant wasn't busy, the cook put money in the jukebox, and we danced."

My twin sister and I stopped wiggling our toes up in front of the rear window and stared at each other. This was a precious historical clue about my mother that she dropped into our laps. My mother and father were the reigning dance stars in our family. We loved to see Mom and Dad dance together, sometimes in our kitchen, sometimes on the porch on warm, lamp-lit nights in Miller Place. Dad was a smooth glider and Mom a serious but graceful follower. Now it appeared that some other man had also held her in his arms.

We passed the General Store in Miller Place. The budding conversation was interrupted by Ingrid's, "We're almost there! We're almost there!"

As if on cue, Ingrid, Eileen, and I started "The Song," our version of the theme from the TV show, *Dragnet*. This was the song that escorted us into our summer paradise, "Dun ta daa, dun ta daa—ta daa, dun ta daa, dun ta daa—ta daa."

This was followed by the front-seat voice of practicality, "We're not there yet. We have to stop at the vegetable stand first."

Fake groans. Secretly, I loved the stop at the vegetable stand. The smell of corn, rhubarb, beans, and dirt was a true signal that we were in the country!

We went the back way through the town of Miller Place, past the musty old library, the little brick school, past the big pond with the weeping willow.

"Wow, look at the tree. It got really big this year." Eileen marked the passing of another year in tree growth.

"Why can't we live in town? Then we could play at the pond." I always seemed to want what was passing me by, forgetting the reward at the end of this journey. The town of Miller Place was really just those few landmarks: a post office, a church, a school, and some houses clustered a little closer together than my grandfather's two houses on the dirt road that was our summer world.

We drove past old Mr. and Mrs. Breschagen's house.

"Think he's still kickin'?" my twin whispered to me.

How did my mother meet the Breschagens? She usually did not make friends easily. Dad was the family's social ambassador, meeting and greeting everyone with a hug, from relatives to the minister's wife.

Both Breschagens had white hair so they must have been ancient. They had no children and lots of grassy property with little pathways just calling for kids to run along. When we visited them, Mom sat on their long outdoor porch and drank lemonade. If Ingrid was in a trying-to-be-a-grown-up mood, she sat on the porch with Mom. My twin and I usually explored the garden paths, narrow dusty pathways that wound in a maze all over the property.

Once we passed the Breschagen's house, it was just a three-minute ride along Woodhull Landing Road and onto the dirt road that led to our summer paradise. Our Summer Song began again in earnest. Then rising up an octave and up in volume with an added bounce as we sat. "DUN TA DAA, DUN TA DAA—TA DAA, DUN TA DAA, DUN TA DAA—TA DAA."

A dirt road with no name marking its existence was the best thing about our piece of Miller Place property. It was set apart from the rest of the world. It was like we were pioneers heading along the rutted road to the new settlement but secure in knowing we had enough provisions in our wagon, and welcoming family at the end of our trail.

We turned in at our driveway, marked by the undernourished cherry tree that struggled up out of the ground like a slanted stairway. Our faces turned left as the car went past the log cabin.

"Who'll be renting the log cabin this year, Mother?" Ingrid asked in her grown-up voice as if she were an accountant in the rent collection. I figured it was really because she was hoping there would be someone her age to play with. She wasn't that interested in playing with dolls anymore.

Whatever will she do on rainy days? She wasn't playing with us, that's for sure. I may have had to share my toys, but I wasn't going to share Eileen with her.

Our Beloved Miller Place House

Up the small rise and:

"Oooh, there it is. I saw the house first! I saw it first."

"Grandpa and Grandma are here. I see their car."

My grandma pushed open the screen door and came down the wooden steps, wiping her hands on the apron that just barely fit around her soft, round body. She didn't play a lot with us or do silly things like other grandmas I had met, but she was always there. She was just there, and that felt good. She was my Red-Ribbon Grandma.

The big white house with red shutters and black trim beckoned to us at the end of the driveway. Our Nassau County house was always talked about as "at home" or "back home." That's where we *lived*. Miller Place was our summer oasis in a year of hard traveling. I believed if I really did have a soul, as Mrs. B. said in Sunday school, then it resided in Miller Place.

Tall oak trees surrounded the house. The pump house and shed sat close by like baby chicks near their mama. The smaller buildings were painted white like the big house, making a matched set, except the pump house was close to the ground with a tiny red hatch door to get down to the pump.

The skinny clothesline, still up from last summer, sagged from the shed to a tree. The shed was where all the tools of our morning chores were kept, along with the toys of summer—beach balls, tire tubes, blankets, badminton rackets and feathery birdies, real wooden croquet mallets, and heavy iron horseshoes. The tools and toys were the proof that our summer promises would be fulfilled.

"We're here!"

Little Finns' Sunday

Chapter Three:

My Finn

Eileen and I had laughing fits about every two days. I called it "giggle glue," and it had us gasping; Eileen even fell on the floor once she was so weak. It was superb! I also called it "Laughing with my Finn."

My Finn is Eileen, my twin sister.

Dad called us "The Finns" because we had Finnish relatives somewhere in Helsinki and because "twin" came out as "finn" for us when we started talking. Most often we were a unit, simply called "The Twins."

We are identical twins. Of course, we looked alike, which we thought was kind of neat. When we stood side by side in front of the bathroom mirror, I saw two skinny girls with the same bony shoulders and Buster Brown haircut. Our eyes are brown and our skin pale in winter and dark brown from the sun in late August. Physically, we were unremarkable, perhaps even plain. What *was* remarkable was that we did look so exactly alike, except Eileen's face was "just a little bit fuller." *How many times would she hear that in her life?*

Imagine waking up every day from the day you are born, and opening your eyes to see two brown eyes like yours looking back at you. The eyes are placed on a face with the same shaped nose that tickles and has to sneeze when you take too big a blob of peppermint toothpaste and a thin-lipped mouth that seems to burst into song just when yours does—"You are my sunshine, my only sunshine ..." All of this is attached to this wonderful best friend, who is always ready to play, talk, hug you, or just sit and hold your hand. This is what being a twin was like for me.

We sounded alike too. Our voices had the same pitch.

"Eileen, come dry the dishes," Mom called.

We looked up from the porch table where we were playing Crazy Eights.

"OK, Mom," I answered, barely able to keep the giggle out of my voice. When I stood up to go into the kitchen, Eileen grabbed my arm.

"You can't fool her with how we look, silly."

I know, but wouldn't that be something? A mother who couldn't tell her twins apart.

Ethel and Eileen With Mom—Five Months

Mom said when we were babies, she tied a ribbon around my wrist to tell the difference. Maybe that's when I started loving colorful ribbons.

When I went to college many years later I figured my Finn and I had greeted each other each morning for almost seven thousand days. My childhood had times of confusion, maybe even moments of fear, but never loneliness.

When we were eight I was curious about family, how we were all related, and ancestors. My mother said we were "offspring of a Finnish father with the Erickson name, and a German mother with the Berberich name, so you were born with a legacy of Scandinavian long winter melancholia." She added, we also had the German Protestant ethic of "work before play." When Mother said this, her voice got kind of funny and breathy like she was going to sneeze, and she looked up at the ceiling. I actually found "melancholia" in the big family dictionary, and it made me think of the cover drawing on the *Jane Eyre* book. Jane's eyes were so big and wide and her face was so long and narrow, with her mouth a thin straight line below her nose. I felt sorry for her having such a sad life. She must have had melancholia too.

My twin, Eileen, and I were always together. My family, including Eileen, called us The Finns, but in my need to possess things—to feel connected—maybe in helping to see who I was, Eileen was *my* Finn. She was so close to me and so much a part of me that I thought of her as *mine*. My Finn was, and still is, my best friend, protector, and audience. And I am hers.

It was not just the looking alike. It was the feeling of having a double—double the feeling of being alive, double the courage, double the fun—and building a rock-solid foundation of who I would be. A foundation that was so strong that even when we were apart, I still had the courage, vitality, and the love of fun.

Mom said we had our own language and signals, even when we were in the playpen. We had this twin connection. We knew when the other was sad or in trouble, even if we were in different places.

We did. We knew.

One summer morning, Finn tripped and fell at Jenkins' patio. I was at home drying the dishes in the kitchen. I suddenly felt this hurt all over my body and started to cry. Sure enough, Finn came home with a scraped knee.

◆   ◆   ◆

Laughing together—that was the best, most delicious connection we had. When we heard something funny, I widened my eyes, we stared at each other, and we laughed until our sides ached.

Laughing with you. Never at you, Finn.

In the magical summers in Miller Place, my Finn and I were together every day from the time we woke up until the time we went to sleep. Even just before sleep, we stretched out together in the big old, saggy double bed and talked.

"Hear the owl? I'm scared," I whispered.

"Don't be a scaredy cat. I'm here."

"Are you asleep yet?"

"Yeah, I'm asleep."

"Do you hear Mom and Dad talking? What does she mean, 'disowned'? We own this house, don't we?"

"No, it's Grandpa's house. Shh, go to sleep."

"I can't. My foot's asleep, but the rest of me isn't. Hey, stop tickling my foot." I started to laugh. "We're supposed to be quiet. Shh." More laughter.

Then we had some "stolen laughter," the laughter you have when you're not supposed to laugh. So, of course, we had to. Like last Sunday. Picture us sitting in church like bookends on either side of my mother. Peeking around Mom and laughing at the funny bald spot on the man's head in front of us, a smooth, open field for a fat, black fly.

We pushed our faces in our pillows when Mother called from the living room, "No more shenanigans now, you two. You should be asleep!"

What are shenanigans? I have to look that up in the dictionary tomorrow.

Eileen was going, "Shenanigans, bananagins" from her pillow.

I had to go to the bathroom, but I already had my allotted bathroom trip.

"Shenanigans bananagins. She-na-ni-gans, Chiquita ba-na-na-gins."

I was asleep.

◆   ◆   ◆

Last Saturday, we had "relative laughter." When someone in our family did something funny or said something weird, we knew it would be rude to laugh out loud at a relative, but we had learned how to create a funny situation out of their actions. That was "relative laughter."

Having Finn as my audience often removed the sharp sting of my mother's criticism.

"Ethel, don't make fun of people," Mom said, as I swung my hips in an exaggerated walk behind my older sister. Looking at Finn smiling at me made it worth Mom's disapproval.

8-53 Miller Place 6 yrs.

Great-Aunt Pauline and Her Nieces

It was raining the Saturday of our relative laughter. It was a steady rain. No wind, so the rain came straight down, hissing through the leaves of the oak trees all around the house. We lowered the green wooden blinds on the screen porch. It was so dark we put the lamps on, right there in the middle of the day. Finn and I were sitting at the big round table playing Crazy Eights with Great-Aunt

Pauline. If you got the angle just right you could look into her huge bifocal glasses to see her cards reflected.

I had heard my old, old Great-Aunt Pauline say, "I laughed till I cried." I had a hard time imagining my forever old great-aunt laughing out loud at just about anything. Sometimes she stayed with us in Miller Place because her husband died, and she was all alone. She seemed happy enough even without Uncle Gary-you-Twins-were-babies-when-he-died. She smiled a lot and even chuckled when she thumped down her cards for a high point hand in canasta. Had she ever laughed where she gasped and held her hand over her chest all bent over and actually snorted? I didn't think so.

Sitting at the table with her Crazy Eights cards fanned in her right hand, Great-Aunt Pauline tapped the long, bony fingers of her left hand and hummed, "What to discard? What to discard?" Her bifocals were at just that right angle for card reflection.

My thought slid out my mouth like spilled milk running across the table and onto the floor. "Why don't you discard that two of hearts, Aunt Pauline?"

Finn was the straight man to my impulsive outburst. She stopped drawing a tic-tac-toe with her fingernail through the embedded dirt of the old plastic table-cloth and looked up. She tried to look very solemn. We stared at each other. A relative laughter session was about to begin. We started to giggle.

"Oh, you Twins, you're rascals."

I took Great-Aunt Pauline's glasses and pulled them down at the end of my nose, joking my way through my confession of cheating. Finn was face down on the table, rolling her head from side to side, shoulders shaking with laughter.

Aunt Pauline wasn't really laughing very loud, but she came out with a "Heh, heh. Oh heh, heh."

◆   ◆   ◆

"Aren't You the Funny One?" laughter took more effort, because the other person had to laugh out loud. I loved to do this one. I had a face I made that was guaranteed to get my Finn going. My special talent was that I could roll my upper lip up under my front teeth, exposing two large front teeth and crooked eyeteeth. Then my lower lip went up and over the bottom teeth so they disappeared. I opened my eyes as wide as I could and gave a nice wet snort from the back of my mouth. This usually happened when we were brushing our teeth before bed. If I did it just as Finn was about to rinse and caught her eye in the mirror over the sink, it was a guaranteed water geyser.

Then she had to say, as toothpaste and water trickled down her chin, "Oh, aren't you the funny one!"

I took pride in the fact that I had also done this cleverly without the snort in church; then it fell into the category of stolen laughter.

Each of these kinds of laughter with my Finn was like a blueprint for what I thought was funny in my lifetime. That laughter tickled my insides and swept a feeling of specialness right to my heart.

Chapter Four:

Starr and Other Beauties

I was probably nine years old when I had my first longing to be beautiful.

I had played with beautiful paper dolls like most little girls did in the 1950s. Finn and I had graduated from cutout Betsy McCall paper dolls and outfits we cut from the old McCall magazines. We moved on to TV and movie star cutouts: Susan Hayward of the glittery evening gowns; June Allyson, who was gorgeous; and my favorite, Mary Hartline, drum majorette of Claude Kirschner's *Super Circus* TV show—Mary, of the pink cheeks and Breck shampoo cascading, blond curls.

I knew Finn and I were doomed to be plain with our mousy brown, straight hair and splotchy summer suntan.

My Finn and I lived vicariously through our paper dolls. We designed new clothes for our paper doll queens by tracing over the cutout clothes, drawing and cutting out new ones, and coloring them in with our Venus "Made in the USA" color pencils. Our beauty queens traveled in wooden block limos to gala parties held under the oak table out on the porch where the tablecloth draped to the floor. Dad's flashlight was the spotlight that followed the stars to the dance floor. Grandpa's flashlight lit up our small ballroom. Susan was glamorous. June was pretty. Mary was sugar and spice.

My red ribbon reminded me that Grandma thought me sweet. But Grandma died when I was seven, and I was left with the red ribbon as a special reminder of her and the safe times on her lap. Sweet was her compliment to my heart, but now I wanted beauty.

Starr Jenkins was beautiful. Starr was the fifteen-year-old friend of my older sister, Ingrid. My sisters and I all had straight "dirty blonde" hair. Starr's honey blonde hair had a natural curl; she had tendrils that seemed to tickle her neck.

Her green almond-shaped eyes were always crinkling with laughter as if she really felt that soft tendril tickle and was delighted by it.

What brought Starr, the butterfly, into our chrysalis world in Miller Place that summer was, of course, the presence of a boy. The boy was my step cousin Hank.

Hank was the nephew of my new step grandmother, Emma. When Grandpa married Emma, it seemed my mother "detested" her at first. Mom called her "that money grabber." But Emma always sang hymns while she washed the dinner dishes and was really nice to Finn and me.

Emma's nephew, Hank, came to spend the summer at Miller Place. Hank was "a hunk" as the older girls said—a six-foot, lanky blond with a twinkle in his eye. He called us "the Squirts." No matter. Quite simply, I loved him.

We had heard late-night conversations drifting in from the porch to our bedroom about Hank being "unmanageable." His mother was mysteriously "gone." His father couldn't handle him.

Hank moved into the old bathhouse on the property. It was part cottage with one showerhead and part storage shed where all the beach gear was kept. During what became known as "The Hank Summer," the tubes, beach towels, and chairs got piled under the porch steps, as baseball and Elvis Presley posters, and a small 45rpm-turntable record player moved into the musty bathhouse with its curtained closet and single bed.

Within one week of Hank's arrival, Starr became his girlfriend.

How did that happen? Did they talk about it and decide? If she sat next to him did that make it happen?

◆   ◆   ◆

The Jenkins lived down the dirt road in a small summer house with two really small bedrooms. One bedroom had bunk beds for the three Jenkins children, Honey, Frankie, and Starr. Honey was our age. Frankie was probably six. He was pretty small and always tagged just slightly behind Honey when we all trooped off somewhere. The fact that Frankie was the fastest runner and most daring tree climber made up for his diminutive size and baby-brother age.

A tiny, stuffy living room, kitchen, bathroom, patio, and a closed-in porch that Mr. Jenkins added on one summer on weekends completed the floor plan at the Jenkins' house. The addition gave them an extra room to move the bunk beds out of the little bedroom, so Starr could have it for herself. It seemed being beautiful also brought the specialness and privacy of having your own room. This would never happen at our house. Privacy was an unknown concept, and besides, none of us were beautiful. Finn and I were replicas of my mother in child-hood—pale and thin—and Ingrid had the blue eyes and square frame of my dad.

My dad spent part of Saturday afternoons helping Mr. Jenkins with the addition. Our dads worked all week at jobs they hated. Then they drove out to the North Shore of Long Island each Friday to spend a short weekend with their families. Sunday evening, they joined the parade of other dad-driven cars trekking back to stale, silent houses near New York City.

Mr. Jenkins and Dad spent one Saturday digging the foundation for the addition, moving cement blocks, and mixing cement for the foundation of that closed-in porch. It was hard, sweaty work, but I remember both dads smiling, shirts hanging over the fence railing, as they drank Rheingold beer and stood in the shade of the big oak tree.

◆   ◆   ◆

More interesting to my budding architectural mind than the Jenkins's porch being built was the loud warning voice Mrs. Jenkins could work up when one of her kids got in trouble. Although Mrs. Jenkins was a pleasant cupcake-baking mom, her piercing, "Frank-ieee! Get in here!" had the power to freeze us all and make my heart feel really funny and heavy. Frankie had again forgotten to do something and was going to get "punished." Our outside play was usually suspended then, because although the punishment was never seen, we could hear Frankie's yelling. Who could have a tea party with that racket going on?

I don't think Starr ever got punished. We all knew Starr was beautiful, and her beauty could save her from being punished. She had what was then known as that Kim Novak look: dark honey-colored hair, sleepy eyes, long eyelashes, and slender legs that went immediately to a dark tan each summer. The boys whistled when she walked to the water's edge at the beach. She was better than our paper doll stars. She was like a real movie star.

Everyone said, "Starr's a beauty, all right."

Looking from Starr to my older sister, Ingrid, I felt a sense of genetic doom. Where Starr seemed carefree and glamorous, Ingrid seemed so serious, plain, and driven. I read and reread *The Ugly Duckling* in hopes of finding a clue that the duckling-to-swan theory worked with girls on Long Island too. I nicknamed Ingrid "The Drudge," because I saw her as such a perfect rule follower and worrier, and that didn't seem like much fun at all.

However, Ingrid was also very powerful. With her four-year lead on us, she was the substitute mother when my parents went out. Although I tried my best not to listen to her, I secretly watched her and wanted to be the big sister. She knew, followed, and felt it was her job to make sure we followed all the rules. She had the pipeline to my mother, to be her confidante during the week while my dad worked in his office.

She was the eyes and ears for rule transgressions. "Mom, Ethel is being fresh again."

"Jeez Louise, I wish Starr was my older sister, not you!"

"Oooh, I'm telling." And off she went.

"Stinky-headed tattle tale," I said, but not very loud.

◆   ◆   ◆

My sibling jealousy was muted by an entire summer of staying at the big house on my grandfather's property. It was as special as living in a castle. It was almost a magical house.

Somehow things were always easier there. We were *free.*

Free from the school year pressure. "Five As and one B. Why didn't you get six As?"

Free from homework. "Work first, then play."

Free from slavish over-obedience to rules.

Free from my mother pacing in the dining room at home as each fading train whistle signaled another commuter train had come and gone and my father wasn't on it. She would sit by the bay window and look down the street as if that would make Dad magically appear. In truth, some nights he stumbled home long after we were in bed.

"What will the neighbors think?" my mother would cry.

Free from Sundays of church dresses that would never be frilly enough to make me feel beautiful.

The Miller Place house and acre of property on the hill was *freedom to experience.*

Freedom to know the thrill of climbing to the very top of Bramenger's tree.

Freedom to race with abandon down Poison Ivy Lane to see the wondrous beach at the end of Woodhull Landing Road.

Freedom to feel the scary excitement of hiding under the crawlspace of the house as Honey shouted, "Ready or not, here I come."

Chapter Five:

Beauty

Usually spying on the big kids held our attention for most of the evening, but that particular night Finn tired of watching teenage hormones rule the group's activities. I was content to watch Starr and Hank all night, unconsciously tilting my head each time Starr tilted hers to look at Hank, until I saw Finn imitating me imitating Starr.

"Shh. Stop moving around. They'll hear us."

"Oh, who cares?" my Finn replied. "They're just doing the same thing they do every night, smoking cigarettes, playing cards, and kissing."

"But look at her hair. You think she curls it at the ends? How come our hair is always crooked in the curling iron? Starr's is like little silky springs. When do you think we'll be beauties?"

"Starr schmar," Eileen sneered. "I've got three more mosquito bites."

She shifted her position in the hydrangea bushes by the porch and proceeded to mark each new bite with the deeply embedded fingernail X. Pressing an X on mosquito bite sites was guaranteed to reduce itching. It hurt so much you didn't feel the itch. This was preferable to the constant scratching that caused a raw smear of broken skin, which left slashes of scratches on our arms and legs each week. Add these to the poison ivy blisters on our ankles from going up and down Poison Ivy Lane each day, and we looked like skinny, diseased orphans.

I sighed.

I'd never be beautiful. I'd never be loved.

◆   ◆   ◆

The only thing that ever made me feel anything near beautiful was the faded silk red ribbon that I used around my ponytail on Sundays or those Saturday nights we went to Port Jefferson. When my hair grew long enough to touch my shoulders, I braided it myself with two rubber bands holding the plaits together. With only one red ribbon, I usually decided to go with the ponytail. I never dreamed of cutting that red ribbon in half for the braids. During the week, I kept my red ribbon in the top dresser drawer in the bedroom, curled up in a really small wad under my socks. If the ribbon got wet, I laid it out on the windowsill next to the screen till it dried, then put it back up in the wad into the drawer. At the end of every summer, I left it in the empty dresser drawer till the next June. Somehow, I knew this talisman to beauty would be safe until the next year—just like everything else in Miller Place.

◆   ◆   ◆

The glow of lightning bugs was too much to hold us to the teenage porch drama. Lightning bugs on a summer evening were like a magic show in the round. Even today, I am still amazed when I look out my patio door on a July evening to see hundreds of twinkling firefly lights, dense in early evening and thinning as they go to sleep later at night. I slide open the screen door to step out and back to the feel of Miller Place.

It was a pretty regular occurrence for us to catch a whole bunch of lightning bugs in glass jars and watch them light up. Maybe it was Honey's little brother, Frankie (who had no idea about anything that resembled beauty), who started the dissecting in order to separate light from bug and see how long they would stay lit. He put the lit parts in the jar, the dull sections dropped and passed over like the girl at a dance in the hand-me-down dress. Eventually, the beauty of the lights faded. Jars were dumped and abandoned in the dust of the dirt driveway, kicked aside by our summer sneakers.

"Beauty fades," my grandmother said.

"But virtue remains," was Great-Aunt Pauline's retort.

Virtue? Like my mother and Ingrid, The Drudge?

I want to be like Starr and never fade.

Chapter Six:

Morning Chores

"Ei-leen and Ethhhh-elll … Come out today?"

Honey's staccato call rang through the woods. It carried across the summer air and down the driveway to the lawn by our white house. This was the signal to see if we were finished with our morning chores.

"Ei-leen and Ethhhh-ell … Come out to play!"

Honey and Frankie were ready to play by nine o'clock every morning. Not so at our house. In spite of the sense of freedom I felt in Miller Place, the work ethic was strictly enforced. If Mother ever did needlepoint, I was sure her pillow would have "Work first, then play" neatly and economically stitched across the front.

All morning we raked, did the dishes, washed the metal glider, and smacked the dust out of its cushions. There were always morning chores. If there weren't outside chores, there were inside chores to reinforce the idea that life was not a twenty-four-hour-a-day picnic. I wondered if that writing my mother did each night was the list for the following day that would save us from the downfall into full-time idleness. Or, maybe our chores provided the contrast that made beach afternoons seem freer by comparison.

My mother had trained a strong work force in her three daughters. That meant six hands each day to make beds, dust ("and the legs of those tables too, young lady"), or wash the crystal in the glass cabinets. The cabinets held a set of heavy pink Depression-glass dishes, ersatz crystal made during the 1930s, and crystal fruit bowls belonging to my grandma. Washing and drying the bowls included glimpses of the rainbow prisms of soft red, orange, green, and blue that glowed as we set them in the sunshine on the porch table to air dry.

Because we were The Twins, my mother assigned jobs to Finn and me as a unit. We were usually the outside workforce; Ingrid, as big sister, got the inside work.

"Just like Cinderella," I smirked as I passed her on our way out into the sunshine day.

My envy of Ingrid being the big sister pulled those bratty remarks out of me. I didn't stop feeling like the little Squirt for years.

◆   ◆   ◆

Even in play, Ingrid could be viewed as either bossy or protective, depending on who was telling the story. When we played with our paper dolls, she often managed to corral all the fancy dresses and evening gowns.

"I'll give you this one," she'd say, pulling out a pale blue Sunday dress for June Allyson.

"No, hey, give me that gold evening gown."

"No."

Maybe that "No" gave Finn and me the motivation to start tracing our cutout doll beauties' meager wardrobes and creating our own.

Morning chores often separated us. Finn and I were outside in the sunshine, yes, but we got the sloppy work also.

Grandpa's Driveway, Gardens, and Whitewashed Rocks

Each summer, one of our first chores was to whitewash the large rocks that lined Grandpa's gardens. He mixed the whitewash powder and water in huge gray metal pails. Off we'd go to one end of the driveway garden.

"Dunk and lift the brush. Slather it on," he directed as he demonstrated the first swipes.

We'd say it with him as he watched us do our first few rocks. "Dunk and lift. Slather it on. Dunk and lift. Slather it on."

When he was satisfied that we were doing it right, he ambled up the hill to actually say good morning to his strawberries. We got "dunk and slather." Red fruit on a vine got an actual greeting. When Grandpa went off to his strawberries we'd get more into the rhythm of it.

"Dunk and lift. Slaaaather it on. Dunk and lift. Sleether-slather it on."

"Hey, don't slather me."

Thick brushes painted each rock that formed a border along the flower gardens on either side of the long driveway.

Whitewashing was popular in most gardens in Miller Place in the '50s. The effect was like painted rocks, but the cost was lots cheaper. The drab rocks became ghostly guardians around the flower gardens so carefully weeded by Grandpa and watered by my Finn and me.

◆   ◆   ◆

Watering the flowers was a twice-weekly chore. We filled the metal watering can at the outside faucet by the kitchen window. It took the two of us holding the handle with the can in between us to lug it up to the driveway. We had learned to step in tandem just through regular walking together; still, a constant trail of water marked our trudging journey. I imagined being the small orphan boy in *Gunga Din* trying to help the thirsty soldiers. Finn and I enacted scenes at either end of our trek.

"For God's sake, get the water, Gunga Din! Waterrrr!"

My time management skills were seeded in that task. Three-hundred steps to the beginning of the drive. Five trips to water one side; five for the other. A forty-minute job, if we were really careful and each plant got saturated. It was thirty minutes, if we just wet the surface.

One July, we had a two-week dry spell with no rain at all. That meant the regular flower watering, and then hauling the pail full to the brim to slake the thirst of the parched strawberries, blueberries, and raspberries at the top of the hill.

My twin sister stopped to rest along the dirt driveway on one of the return trips.

"Finn, look. The raspberries are ripe. They're ready to be picked."

We put the watering pail down to bend over to look at the vines. Picking ripe raspberries was not a chore. It happened almost on its own.

"Ethel, look. You don't even have to pull the berry off the vine." Finn gave just a gentle tug with her thumb and forefinger, and the berry fell off into her hand. She popped it into her mouth, and I watched a smile close around it: snack time. Oh, the delicious taste of a burst of soft sweetness of a summer raspberry in your mouth!

◆   ◆   ◆

Maybe our chores took all morning because of the adventures that happened along the way. Take raking. Raking was a weekly job, along the side of the driveway from the outdoor stone fireplace down to the old wooden outhouse and garbage pit. The raking covered a plot of land measuring about fifty feet across and four-hundred feet long from the fireplace to the garbage pit. Any number of dangers could befall us.

Although we had no pets, our neighbors did. The Mitchell's and Kooney's dogs, out for their morning run, became "Wild Dog Pack coming."

"Head for the Sunday Climbing Tree." Finn and I both had a great sense of drama. "It's our only escape from gnashing teeth and threatening growls."

Safe up on the long limb of our favorite tree, we ate small apples to ward off the effects of any possible canine-inflicted injuries.

"All clear. Down to the birdbath."

The small cement birdbath lake was hosting a ladybug-bathing contest.

"Finn, you be the judge today. Get down to eye level." I lowered my voice to sound like the TV announcer. "We'll see which preening orange beauty is the winner."

Finn's thumb and pointer finger gently plucked the winning ladybug off the edge of the birdbath and placed it on a neighboring snow blossom bush. The sad and unsuspecting runner-up and losers got flicked into the pool at the center to see who could swim.

"Tidal wave," Finn signaled to me. Water rushed through the watering can spout into the bowl and wiped out the entire bug population.

◆   ◆   ◆

The spider check of the outhouse was next. Our imaginations warned that poisonous spiders might decide to venture into the outhouse. Our chore was to brush out the cobwebs and spiders so the outhouse was readied for "emergencies." Emergencies were announced by the loud clunking that came from the well in the pump house, signaling a loss of water supply to our bathroom. Then, the outhouse was our toilet, and the outside hand pump was our water supply until a plumber came and disappeared down into the pump house to do noisy hammering battle that brought the water back again.

The wooden outhouse was built forever ago, back in the 1930s when there was no indoor plumbing at all. It was known as "a three-seater"—big enough to have a bench with two adult holes and one smaller hole for kids. The bench covered a ditch. A roll of stiff toilet paper resided on the shelf, and pale yellow paint coated the walls and seat in a futile attempt to give it a homey touch. That yellow paint allowed all the spider webs to be in full view.

"Think spiders can smell things?" Finn wondered as we looked around. We looked at the smaller seat with a mix of disgust and curiosity.

Then we arrived at the cause-and-effect connection. If our pump house pump actually broke, *we'd* have to use the outhouse.

Finn made a further connection to Mom's childhood. Sitting on the smaller opening, she said, "If this was built in the olden days before they had a bathroom, Mom actually sat right here when she was a little girl."

At dinner that night, the conversation steered from whitewashing rocks to who painted the inside of the outhouse. It seemed only fitting for me to ask the next question.

"Mom, did you really have to go out there? What if it was the middle of the night?"

"I took the old lantern and walked out."

"Alone?"

"Yes." Mother budgeted her words as carefully as she did money, leaving me to wonder why *her* mother didn't walk her out there. With this bit of information came the understanding that the same lonely walk would be mine if Finn wouldn't go with me.

Next morning, I even counted the 435 steps from the white house to the outhouse. Then, I walked it with my eyes squinted almost closed, just in case I had to make the trip some disastrous night and there were no flashlights.

◆   ◆   ◆

Honey's signal of "Ei-leen and Ethhhh-elll..... . Come-out-today?" called us back to chores. Once chores were done, we were free.

"Quick, rake all those leaves and twigs to the garbage pit. Rake hard on the ground. Grandpa'll come by and look to see those rake lines."

The garbage pit was a hand-dug hole about six feet deep and eight feet square. We threw all paper and decomposable garbage into it daily to be burned at night, an odorous bonfire that we all went out to watch.

Sometimes, particularly after weekend cookouts, the damp corncobs and left-over limp salad made the pile too wet, and we crumpled up newspaper for kindling. Dad lit the fire.

One time, Ingrid, being the oldest, was allowed to start it. Dad and Finn and I watched as she lit the match and held it next to a newspaper-twisted torch.

"Oooh," she kind of squealed, jumping back and dropping it down into the hole. The used paper plates and cups caught, sending up small glowing bits of paper and ashes. The smell of burning paper, wood, and watermelon rinds filled the air.

If I ever get to do it, I'll hold that torch until the last possible second—

"Here, Ethel, try this." Dad handed me a smaller torch already edged with glowing red edges. I took it without looking at him.

—So it will be like a ball of flame.

I held it and held it before hurling it down into the waiting pit. It roared for a few seconds like a volcano. I could feel the heat on my face and turned to feel the cool night air, then back to the heat again. Add some of these old napkins.

Dad's voice brought me back to the pit.

"Ethel, stop throwing all that extra paper in. That's enough now. You want to set those trees on fire?"

Part of me did, just to see how it would look.

Chapter Seven:

Clearing Poison Ivy Lane

For one entire Saturday morning in early June, my father and Mr. Jenkins were rural trailblazers. With grass scythes over their shoulders, they strode down the dirt road in back of our houses toward the woods. It was the annual clearing of Poison Ivy Lane. All of us little kids trailed behind, dancing in anticipation of the reclaiming of the path.

Both dads were stocky and used to physical work, even though their weekdays were spent at desks in offices in the city. Saturday mornings on Long Island were devoted to outside work—cutting tree limbs, repairing fences, painting, chopping wood.

Afternoons were filled with swimming and playing with us kids in the water at the beach. My dad never seemed to tire of "flipping" any kid who lined up in the water. Squatting down and cupping his hands in the water in front of him for a foothold, he'd smile a big smile.

"You ready for this?"

Each kid had a turn to put one foot in Dad's handmade pocket, put both hands on his shoulders facing him, and start that little jump.

"One two … three!" we'd all shout.

On "three" Dad pushed the foothold up out of the water, and up the flipper went, jumping as high up as they could in the foothold. Then a push up and out away from him into the water. It was a really good flip if you went totally up and out of the water before the descent to splashdown.

I liked to think Dad was so strong solely because of us. You could see the muscles in his arms glistening when he tossed the kids in the water. When he stood on the beach and held his arms up like the strong man in the circus and extended each forefinger, Finn and I reacted to that extended forefinger signal like Pavlov's dogs. We'd grab onto his whole fist, and he'd lift us up and down—to our delight and everyone who watched.

◆   ◆   ◆

But first—clearing Poison Ivy Lane. Poison Ivy Lane was a narrow swath of space through a dense woods. The trees and underbrush were so thick it was like an overcast day when we walked through the woods. A year's growth of poison ivy covered the ground, trees, and an old chain link fence along the woods. The lane cut the walk time to the beach. The boring way was a half-hour walk down and around the bend of the sun-softened, tarred Woodhull Landing Road. The exquisite way was a mere ten minutes through Poison Ivy Lane and down a sandy road to the glorious beach on the Long Island Sound.

We were forbidden to go through the woods until the dads had cut down a year's growth of the shiny, but poisonous three-leafed plants. They'd wade through in khaki pants and boots, swinging the scythes. First my dad, then Mr. Jenkins, would slash the leaves down to the ground. Bits of greenery would fly. Dad stopped occasionally and wiped off the blade with his Army-Navy work gloves. Frankie, the only boy in the neighborhood near our age that summer, carried the beer cans in an old plaid plastic cooler.

"Frankie, hand me a clean one." An empty can came sailing over Mr. Jenkins's shoulder. Frankie jockeyed in back of him to catch it and toss back a full one, as his dad turned for the catch with a big grin on his face.

Job division by gender was a given. The year I was ten, I had read every *Little House* book I could find, and felt like Laura watching Pa go off across the wilderness as we "womenfolk" stayed at the top of the path and watched "our men" disappear downhill and around the curve into the wilderness.

"Bye, Pa," I called, swept into my *Little House* fantasy.

Once a single lane path had been cut, my dad or Mr. Jenkins, emboldened by a few Rheingold beers, went back to the house and started up the gasoline hand mower to "just run 'er through once to clear this mess."

Ivy, stones, sticks, and twigs spurted out of the mower in little explosions as it bumped down the path. The debris threatened, but never succeeded, in defeating the small motor. Honey, Eileen, and I dragged rakes down the path to clear the cut leaves and vines off to the sides where they piled up, waiting to get soggy from that night's thunderstorm.

At the other end of the lane, we pushed the final pile into the woods, while the dads took all the tools back up to the house.

"All clear," Mr. Jenkins shouted to Mrs. Jenkins as he pushed the mower into their storage shed. Frankie was off the patio like a shot, slamming the kitchen door as he went to put on his bathing suit.

"Yes. Go. Get ready." Dad knew what we wanted.

Twenty-five minutes later we were heading down Poison Ivy Lane—the opening ceremony to playtime. Chores were done. Dad had served his famous PB & J (heavy on the J that day because my mother was changing the beds) sandwiches for lunch, and then the Squirts set off.

Frankie and Honey were already waiting at the top of the cleared lane. "Ready?" asked Frankie.

Navigating down Poison Ivy Lane was an adventure in itself. Single file, Frankie, as the leader set the pace, meandering at first to see what was new that June, breaking the thin spider webs that stretched across the path, hopping onto uncovered stones. The final stretch required racing so fast the momentum of going downhill eliminated all brake power. We had to skid to a halt at the end of the woods so we didn't bump into his mom who had started ahead of us.

All of us kids got our annual poison ivy rash, which resulted in calamine polka dots on our legs, fierce scratching, X'ing, and another of my mother's mantras echoing behind us: "You'll be scarred for life if you keep that up."

There was a short space of about a hundred feet at the end of the lane. This crossed the Red and White House property. Once out of the dark woods, it always surprised me to find the sun blazing at the other end. The Red and White House was occupied all those years, and yet we never talked to the people who lived there. We just called it "The Red and White House." We pretended we couldn't be seen. Decades of kids had cut across the Red and White's property, and no one ever said, "Hey, you kids, get off my land." But the possibility of this occurring kept the risk and daring factor of this part of our journey alive.

We could roam till suppertime, and where we roamed was The Beach.

Chapter Eight:

A Summer Portrait

My idols for beauty in 1958 were the Breck Shampoo girl, the Rheingold Beer girls, and my precious movie-star paper dolls. Ingrid's friend, Starr, was my real, live teenage beauty. But the epitome of adult beauty in my preadolescent life was wrapped up in a living icon known as Mrs. Desmaisons.

Suzanne Desmaisons lived in a small, pristine summer cottage up the hill from the beach. Where our house was big and open with bare floors, her wooden floors were covered by little "throw" rugs. That always made Finn and me laugh. How could anyone imagine throwing rugs at Mrs. Desmaisons'?

Our laughter was lost on my mother. "Shh, don't be rude!"

Plain white sheer curtains bordered our glass windows. Crisp curtains with tiny paisley designs embraced her windows. Our gardens were bordered by chunky whitewashed rocks. Her gardens had little iron benches alongside, and the pathways were layered with tiny white pebbles. We didn't run along her pathways. We also wore dresses even though it wasn't church. It was better than church. Finn and I walked arm in arm as slowly and gracefully as we imagined two princesses would.

In the cluster of moms who dressed in bright print bathing suits and short terrycloth cover-ups, Mrs. Desmaisons shone like a mature polished jewel. Most summer mothers wore Woolworth sunglasses and colorless lip balm at the beach. Mrs. Desmaisons wore red lipstick—at the beach! Her brilliantly blue eyelids were protected by sunglasses that had little sparkly jewels at the outer edges. Her short silver hair was tucked neatly under a turban as she sat beneath a small beach umbrella in her solid dark-red, one-piece bathing suit. It seemed she had every color suit—from vivid red to chic black, pale yellow, even pink. Her nails were shaped like ovals and smoothly color-coordinated with the suit of the day. Mrs. Desmaisons was my introduction to Bain de Soleil and Chanel Number 5.

Suzanne Desmaisons was French.

She established my lifelong romance with the glamour of Paris, France, and anything French.

Mrs. Desmaisons's daily entrance on the beach was a premier walk-on. She paused at the top of the ramp on the hill, bringing one hand to shade her eyes under the brim of her straw sunhat.

Although not more than 5'1" tall, she held herself so straight she seemed tall. Her walk added credence to the practice of walking with a book on your head for good posture.

When she began her regal descent, the fringe from her black gossamer beach poncho rippled around her like small subjects surrounding their queen.

"Here she comes," one of us announced.

Finn, Honey, Frankie, and I turned as one to watch. She would glide down the ramp with some young, or not so young, admirer carrying her wooden picnic basket and sun umbrella.

She herself carried her straw beach tote over one arm. Her low beach chair was placed on her SD monogrammed beach towel like a throne. After sitting, she carefully emptied her beach bag—book, jeweled reading glasses, thermos, and suntan oil were gently laid out on the separate small towel next to her beach towel. She always sat at a slight angle to the water. As an adult, I would replicate this setting many times at the beach.

Mrs. Desmaisons was like other summer women in that she stayed alone in her house during the week. Her husband, Louis, pronounced "Lou-ieee," appeared from some fascinating profession and joined her at the beach on weekends.

"I bet he's a diplomat at the UN," Finn whispered as we stared without embarrassment one Sunday afternoon.

"Or a clothing designer," I added, thinking of the ideas he would have for my cut-out dolls.

"Maybe he's even the owner of Chanel!" breathed Honey.

"Ah, Lou-ieee," Mrs. Desmaisons smiled at him from her seated throne.

"Ma Suzanne," he'd say, gazing at her, eyes crinkling at the corners with delight.

"Suzanne. Lou-iee." My twin whispered their treasured first names as if to say them any louder would break the spell of glamour that drifted around Mrs. Desmaisons.

The only similarity with other summer moms was the absent husband. Mrs. Desmaisons was at least ten years older than the other moms, yet seemed ageless. Their only child, Louis Jr., was called "Young Lou-ieee" and was not as young as we. He was old enough to drive.

At least once during the week, Young Louis could be seen waving from the top of the sand dunes and then moving gracefully down the ramp to the beach. Where everyone else thumped or ran down the ramp, Louis Jr. moved deliberately and lightly, almost on the balls of his feet. He always greeted us as he moved by our clump of kid beach blankets.

"'Allo, ladies."

In my mind I envisioned my hair swirling in slow motion away from my face and across my shoulder as I smiled shyly, yet with a hint of boldness, in silent reply. In actuality, he probably was greeted with three openmouthed gawking girls and one belching boy as he went by.

His mother remained seated as he bent over to give her not one, but two kisses, one on each cheek.

How did they know which cheek to do first? When my Finn and I tried it, she always turned into my mouth and we ended up bumping jaws.

Mrs. Desmaisons was a mermaid at the water's edge. Her swim began by slowly wading from the shoreline in up to her knees. She dipped one hand in the water and brought it to the opposite shoulder and down her arm, acclimating limb by limb to the water's temperature. First left arm, then right. We watched entranced.

"Will that be all today or will she swim?" Honey asked.

Honey, Finn, and I turned on our towels to watch and learn.

If it was to be a swim day, she waded in farther, up to her chest, and then leaning to her right side, she slid into the water.

"OK, there she goes. She's going in."

Cupping her right hand in the water, she pushed out with the left arm. Turning her head to the side out of the water, her mouth opened in a small round "O" as she slowly exhaled with the push. Her petite feet flicked with a slight flutter kick, and she was launched like a graceful new canoe out from the shoreline. It was from Mrs. Desmaisons I learned of the breaststroke.

Eileen, Honey, and I spent many hours perfecting the Mrs. Desmaisons Swim.

"'Allo, watch me!" we'd call to one another in soprano-pitched voices.

Our idol swam left to right, from our beach buoy to the boundary of the public beach, and then back. Then, she slowly swam in, rose out of the water like a water nymph, and walked in a meandering kind of way back to her blanket.

The post-water part of her swim consisted of carefully drying her arms, then legs. She patted her face with a smaller towel. Then, while sitting, she dried her feet. Drying done, her beautification was accessorized. We witnessed the reapplication of lipstick, with her lips open, then pressed together as she tilted her head to view her face in a tiny, round mirror.

By then we had drifted over toward her towel on our way to reenact the swim, catching a whiff of her heaven-scent Bain de Soleil.

"Hi, Mrs. Desmaisons."

"Hi, Mrs. Desmaisons."

"Hi, Mrs. Desmaisons."

She paused with jeweled sunglasses in hand, so we got a full glance of those flashing eyes.

"'Allo, mas petites."

This greeting dissolved us into a mass of girlish arms clasping each other as we staggered into the water with the weight of such a loving hello.

We turned back by the shore to get one final look. Leaning back and stretching her arms overhead marked the last act of our idol's swim performance. As she lowered her arms in slow motion, her contented sigh coincided exactly with the moment her fingers touched down on the sand at her sides.

Ahh!

Chapter Nine:

No-Chores Saturday

One Saturday morning, my dad came up from the half-basement where he had a workbench. In his hands he held three diamond-shaped wooden frames.

"Let's go fly kites!" he decreed with a big smile on his face.

This was extraordinary. Usually Dad spent Saturday morning doing his chores. He worked all week at his office and drove out to Miller Place on Friday nights, which must have been an eternally long trip without us singing in the back of the car. Then, each Saturday morning he was outside, whistling and chopping wood for the outside stone fireplace or cutting the grass.

But not this Saturday. This Saturday it would be kites!

My sisters and I threw damp dishtowels over the little rack by the kitchen door.

"What about those breakfast dishes?" came my mother's call back to chores.

"Mom," I begged. "Dad?" A plea for intervention.

Mom and Dad had this kind of silent back and forth negotiation. At home, Mom's call back to schedules was supreme. In Miller Place, she was different—easier, softer.

"OK, OK." We got our reprieve.

One quick pull on the carved woodpecker knocker by the kitchen, and my sisters and I were out the screen door.

"Don't slam the door," came my mother's behavior reminder. My mother was the queen of don'ts. "Don't slam the door." "Don't talk with your mouth full." "Don't talk back." "Don't give me that look, young lady."

◆   ◆   ◆

Playtime with my dad was easy fun. When Mom was worrying about money, he'd grab her around the waist and hum "dancing cheek to cheek." Sometimes it worked, and she'd start laughing and they'd spin around the kitchen. Those were the times I knew my parents were in love.

Dad was always in love with my mother. He loved most people. If he loved you, there would never be a time when he didn't love you. I could be sulking, or answer back, or forget something, and was still sure of his love. With Mom, it was different. Sulking, answering back, were things that just came out of me without planning. Those were things that could make my mother physically pull back or turn away from me. Somehow, I felt that she was pulling back on her love too.

Sometimes, Mom moved away from Dad too. Sometimes she pushed away from the dance invitation. That push was powerful, not physically, but for a quick second a look of little-boy hurt would sweep across his face. Next second, he'd be helping her with the dishes or, better yet, turn to one of us and dance. If it was me, I'd put my feet on top of his soft moccasins, playing Ginger Rogers to his Fred Astaire.

◆   ◆   ◆

This Saturday, Dad had made three wooden kite frames. He had three rolls of gift-wrap paper under one arm and an old white sheet balled up under the other arm. Now this was very odd; with three kids and never enough money, gift giving in my family was only at Christmas and birthdays.

Dad laid the rolls of paper on the stoop.

Where did he get that paper?

My Finn covered her frame in white paper with purple lilacs. "I can just smell the lilacs," she said holding her kite up to her nose and grinning.

In a move of twin separation, I made a choice different from Finn's. "I'm using this one, the one with red, orange, and yellow. The whole world will see mine."

Ingrid's was red and white stripes. We tied strips of torn sheet on the string tails, and Dad attached strong white cord to the crossbars.

We orbited around Dad, up the driveway, down the hill, and across to the field that was on the other side of the dirt road. I held my kite up overhead in the field, with Dad holding the ball of cord. We were ready to fly. Dad started unwinding the string, backing away across the makeshift softball field he and Mr. Jenkins had cleared for the big kids.

I held my sunshine diamond high up over my head.

"Stand right there." Dad kind of jogged backwards. Then he was going faster and faster, his tan legs pumping up and down.

"Let go! Let go!" he shouted.

I did, and the wind pulled the kite up and out of my hand. It wobbled and then caught. It went swooping crazily in the air till the breeze lifted it on its own. Up, up it went.

"Here," Dad called. "Take the cord. Fly it."

His hands stayed over mine. We let out the string in tandem. When he stepped away, I was on my own. My kite went up higher than any birds had ever been over the field. It took my breath away. We all looked up.

"Now, me." Finn called Dad over.

I was left in my patch of the field, bare feet on the sandy dirt, but the rest of me was up with my kite.

"How beautiful," I whispered to myself, but beautiful in a way I had never thought of or felt ever before.

We flew kites for several weekends that summer. On a good flying day, I could get the kite up by myself and let the string out till the kite was no more than a speck in the blue sky.

Ahhh, it felt grand! Yet it was never as magical as that first sunny No-Chores Saturday.

Chapter Ten:

Rutti Tut Tut, Zee Zee-Zee Zee Trot Trot, and Lady Beaver Stream

There were several summers when our lives were taken over by the whims and orders of a four-and-a-half-foot tall boy named Tommy. The log cabin was rented by the Mackinneys, Mr. and Mrs., and their son, Tommy. Tommy was a little older than Ingrid, and had "I'm the Boss" written all over him. Finn and I were in awe of this boy who wasn't a tagalong like Frankie and also wasn't so out of reach like Hank would be in later years. We obeyed him without question.

His parents encouraged his independence like a mama and papa bear preparing their cub for the first winter alone. His father rigged up a basket pulley in the tree by their porch. On sunny days, his mother hoisted his lunch up to him. He sat swaying near the top, his thick blond curls lifted by the breeze, his strong tanned legs up in the V of the branches, basket on his lap, as he ate his ham and cheese on rye.

The summer Finn and I were five, Tommy was the eleven-year-old Indian chief of the acre, leading my sisters and me as his three Indian braves in enactments of ceremonies from his imagination. His father put up a huge green canvas tent, tall enough for all of us to stand in, and secure enough with a wooden floor so Tommy could sleep in it at night in his sleeping bag.

"By yourself?" I asked.

"'Course."

"You're not afraid?"

He sneered. "'Course not."

"Wow." I never did anything by myself. I always had Finn.

Tommy was the chief of our tribe, naming us with an authority that came from just a few days of sensing our obedience.

"Stand before me, my braves. Receive your tribal names." Tommy wore this great big headdress with pink and purple and bright green feathers down the back.

We faced our Chief, our sneakers moving like soft-skinned moccasins padding across the wooden tent floor. Skinny, but tall and proud, we lined up. Ingrid, Eileen, and Ethel.

"Ingrid, you are now, and will be known forever as, Rutti Tut Tut."

Ingrid smiled; her face shone with pride.

"Eileen, take the name of Zee Zee-Zee Zee Trot Trot."

All those tricky words for one small kid. I looked at my Finn. Another name—would I be able to call her that?

"Ethel, you are Lady Beaver Stream."

"What? Lady Beaver Stream? What kind of a name is that? What about Princess Beautiful Stream?"

"No." Our Chief turned away. "Let the Naming Dance begin."

I wasn't happy about the Beaver Stream part but liked that title of Lady.

Emboldened with our native names, our quiet footfalls became thuds, then louder, stamping on the wooden floor in the tent in that dirt yard by the log cabin. Oh, it was glorious! We stamped and jumped until my bangs were wet with sweat. We chanted our names—first slow and soft like whispers of grass in the field, then loud, and faster and faster! We shouted our names as loud as we could!

"Stop! Sit!"

We sat cross-legged in our line. One by one, we drank from the canteen of cool water Chief Tommy held over our upturned, open mouths. The water dribbled in my mouth, trickled coolly down my neck, and under the collar of my T-shirt. Could any Indian kids have more fun than this?

◆   ◆   ◆

One Saturday afternoon, my sisters and I were on our screen porch, silently coloring by numbers with our Venus pencils. The only sounds were the soft *swish swish* of the pencils on paper, so it was easy to hear the Indian call of our Chief.

"Whoo-ooo, whoo-ooo, whooo-oooo." Tommy's Indian call made us lift our heads like it was a prairie dog alert. What made us grab the pencils as we ran to the tent?

After initiating us into the day's tribal meeting by drawing brownish designs on our arms with Indian rocks dipped in water, Ingrid leaned back to admire her work.

"A bit of color is what we need," she pronounced, and so Rutti Tut Tut carefully applied beautiful designs to our faces. She chose the Venus pencils with care: yellow, green, red, and my favorite, aquamarine.

Then we circled 'round and 'round in the tent whooping, "Aieeee! Aieee! Rutti Rutti! Zee-Zee! Zee-Zee! Lady Lady!" and stamping our feet in what was our best imitation of an Indian Color Ceremony.

It was only when the ceremony had ended and we went back to the white house porch that we realized the seriousness of using Venus Made in the USA Color Drawing Pencils on our skin. The Venus colors did not rinse off with our Chief's canteen water. Scrubbing our faces only made the bright Venus colors look more vibrant.

It was unfortunate this all happened on the weekend. We were used to getting in trouble with my mom. We had developed the thick cocoon kids spin to deflect the voice of punishment from the daily family disciplinarian. We knew the "wait till your father gets here" was useless if the bad behavior happened on Monday or Tuesday. By Friday evening, it was too long ago to work up any sufficient, righteous anger.

More likely, the transgression just got an annoying mention. "The Twins forgot the glider cushions, and they got all wet in the thunderstorm." Since Dad might be sitting on the formerly abandoned cushions, and they were now clean and dry, what kind of punishment could be worked up from that?

My mother could be a fiercesome yeller. She was also a great martyr, so when we came whooping onto the porch that Saturday, rainbowed with Venus pencil drawings on our faces and arms, she took to the wicker couch with her one hand on her forehead, moaning and glaring at the same time, "What did I do to deserve such trouble?"

To be in trouble when Dad was around was a different story. My father did not yell when he was angry. He got very quiet and talked to us as if we were grownups.

Finn and I got a dose of his "disappointment" in us about the Venus pencils, which was harder than any punishment, especially since he sat right across from us at eye level, and I could see that his eyes *were* just dripping with disappointment. I felt my lips quiver with remorse. That was hard punishment.

Ingrid got much worse.

We heard Dad talking very quietly to her. "You are the older sister. I count on you to be responsible. You are responsible for The Twins. What if something was in those pencils that could hurt them?"

Was it this kind of responsibility that made my older sister such a strict rule follower? It seemed to cause her such anguish when she was a teenager. Other kids had rebellions of smoking and drinking beer at parties. Not her. She was often alone on Friday nights, when other girls were dating. Yet, it seemed to serve her well in later years, when she and her husband guided and protected their own children with clear, parental conversations.

Back then, however, Ingrid cried and cried, not because of her vision of Finn and me, deformed and having our skin falling off our faces from the potential Venus skin-poisoning. Not at all. She cried and cried because she had disappointed my father.

Years later, I smile at the memory, still feeling the excitement of our tent ceremony. Ingrid smiles too, but her closing statement is, "Yeah, but remember how angry Dad was about those Venus pencils?"

Not me. I keep Lady Beaver Stream, Rutti Tut Tut, and Zee Zee Trot Trot dancing in line in my head, in the circle of Tommy's wild, but fun ideas.

Chapter Eleven:

Polaroid Summer

When the Claretons rented the log cabin, they came with their two boys. Ernie was the same age as Finn and me, and James was his skinny, younger brother.

Mr. Clareton usually had some sort of new toy for "his boys." Looking back, I realize Mr. Clareton included himself in the "boy" category. He loved the toys just as much as his sons did, and all us kids got the benefit of his generosity. One year, it was fireworks on the Fourth of July; another year, it was a Polaroid camera.

A Real Train Set!

The most extravagant was the summer of the real outdoor train set.

The train tracks circled the same area where Tommy's Indian tent had been years before.

The set was small enough to fit in the dirt yard, but big enough for us to crouch in the metal train cars and take a ride.

The outdoor train set drew us to the log cabin every weekend of that summer. The air felt soft and heavy as evening shadows gathered like waiting passengers around the train tracks. The boys slammed out of the tiny log cabin porch as their dad pulled off the heavy tarp that covered the trackside control box.

"First trip comin' up," he'd shout. "Who's in the first car?" First car meant you were the leader. You decided where the trip was going. Ernie was usually first. Privileges of being the oldest child were accepted without complaints.

As the train pulled around at the end of his loop, our faces turned to Ernie. He looked at me.

"OK, Ethel, now you go first."

I climbed on. I could just fit my ten-year-old body in the car. I had to stretch my legs out to the sides of the engine car to be able to sit. It wasn't comfortable but it was really neat!

"All passengers aboard." I called out. "Express to—New Yooork City!"

We all shouted, "Hooray!"

The train went around the railroad yard, past the log cabin town, through the two-tree forest, and under the clothesline bridge. The train wheels clacked faster and faster. When I was a spectator, the little train just chugged along, but from that first car engineer's seat, it seemed like we whizzed around.

◆   ◆   ◆

I associated the Clareton years with being rich. Maybe this was because I was getting to be aware of the world outside Miller Place. It seemed to be a fact that if you had a lot of money you could buy things that were fun, not just boring like dish detergent, toilet paper, and socks. This went beyond special treats like fifteen-cent ice cream cones or ice cream sundaes at Gramma's.

In my family we never talked about buying toys, and here Ernie and James had their own train in the yard, and just for the summer, not even all year round. Imagine what they had the other months of the year. Imagine birthdays! Imagine Christmas!

"Let's fix it so we can live with them for the winter too," I begged Finn.

"I don't want to live with two boys," she replied.

"But there's something interesting about boys," I said, as I eyed James poking his big brother, Ernie, in the backside with a croquet mallet.

We lived in a house dominated by our mother. Our world at the beach was filled with moms and kids, but the boys were starting to stand out as ... different. They had a recklessness, a kind of rocketing energy, I was attracted to.

◆   ◆   ◆

One morning, at breakfast, James didn't get first pick at the pancake platter. Finn and I were raking leaves up by the stone fireplace, so we were in hearing distance of the breakfast dish clatter and conversation.

"I wanted that one," I heard him whine.

"Wait your turn," his mother said in a low voice.

What happened next thrilled me because it was so unheard of in my family. He *yelled* at his mother! His voice rose to almost a scream. "I hate you!" he shouted and ran outside, slamming the screen door really loud.

Finn and I moved closer by the big stones of the fireplace to watch. His mother rushed to the screen door and then paused, one hand holding it partway open. Her face actually looked like it got dark and her eyebrows wrinkled together.

"No TV for you tonight, young man," she said in her low voice, but it was also a very serious voice. She closed the door without a sound and went back to the kitchen.

Now that gave me something to think about. A punishment of no TV seemed worth it to make an exit like that and really slam a door! We didn't even have a TV in Miller Place.

"You want to live with that?" was Finn's comment. Her reasoning was, "Besides, Ernie's not good at climbing trees, or running, or other outdoor stuff, and James is just a tag-along."

Keeping my eyes on James as he kicked dirt at the train engine, I tried to boost my argument for an address change. "But Ernie's very smart and uses really big words, even with us, not just in front of grown-ups. Remember when I chased after a run away ping-pong ball, and he said, 'Aren't they elusive!'"

James disappeared around the side of the house and I heard him go in the screen door of the side porch. "Mom?" He and his voice disappeared back into his family.

"I laughed and laughed because he's so goofy, but we did get Mom's dictionary out to look up the word just to make sure he wasn't insulting me. 'Elusive: skillfully evasive.' Then I had to follow the word trail to look up evasive. 'Evasive: tending to escape; elude.' Again, down the dictionary trail. 'Elude: avoid capture.'"

"Well ...," started Finn.

"Now, *that* was kind of clever," I admitted, "but I wasn't going to tell that to Ernie."

"No living with those boys," Finn answered in Mom's "Don't ask me again" voice.

Well, if Finn wouldn't live with the Claretons, neither would I, because I would never be separated from Finn.

◆   ◆   ◆

During the Polaroid summer, Mr. Clareton took lots of pictures of us kids. My albums today still hold faded pictures of gawky, tanned kids eating ice cream at the beach, riding the train, and posing by the fireplace at Sunday cookouts. I became aware of what I looked like even more from the photos than comparing myself to my Finn. I was wearing my hair longer, past my shoulders, pulled back in a ponytail or braids. Every activity became a black-and-white Polaroid memory, a piece of evidence to scrutinize how I looked without anyone telling me I was too vain.

No other adult we knew had a Polaroid camera. It was like magic. You didn't have to take the film to the general store for them to send away to the developing company. You didn't have to wait a week to get the pictures back. You pulled out the paper tab from the camera, and if you could wait only sixty seconds, peeled away a small black-and-white photograph.

One Sunday cookout evening while we were waiting for the burgers to be done, Mr. Clareton popped the Polaroid in front of us.

"Smile."

The flashbulb made a really bright flash and POP! noise. He pulled out the film, and left it on the table with directions to wait those sixty seconds. Here's where the magic began. As we stared and stared at that small rectangle, dark images began to emerge. We could actually see the picture forming, only in reverse.

"Ooh, here it comes," We all waited and watched when he finally pulled the backing off the picture and the chemical smell rose up as he carefully rubbed the fixer glue on the glossy photo.

His warning of "Don't touch it now, it's sticky," were the magnetic words to make James and me reach out tentative fingers as he turned to throw away the backing. It *was* sticky. James was left literally holding the paper, shaking his hand trying to get it off while the rest of us stood in innocent witness.

Today, I think of the seventy digital pictures I took at my niece's birthday party, instantly deleting twenty of them. I am struck by the blasé acceptance my eight-year-old great-niece shows of this miracle of capturing likeness. But I see the same close-up interest in looking at herself that was in me fifty years ago.

Fireplace Beauties

Back then, I also leaned my elbows on the table to get a closer look. There, standing by the stone fireplace, were two suntanned girls with white midriff shirts, necklines stretched out across their skinny shoulders, hands folded in front of them. The girl with the ponytail wore a pearl necklace and looked kind of excited and wide-eyed. *It was me!* Maybe I wouldn't have to curl my hair around pencils or brush it a hundred strokes every night. I looked real and happy and almost pretty in that Polaroid.

Maybe, just maybe, all this growing up stuff was actually going to happen to me.

Chapter Twelve:

The Field

The overgrown field had been along one side of the road as far back as I could remember. On one side of the dirt road were all the summer houses. Our summer neighbors along the sand-colored dirt road were the Bramengers, the Mitchells, the Kooneys, the Jenkins, and the mysterious Bobson family down at the end by Poison Ivy Lane.

On the other side of the dirt road was this huge weed-infested, daisy-and-goldenrod-filled field. The weeds grew higher than my head, a scratchy forest in themselves. We Squirts could get lost in the field, breaking off daisies for ragged bouquets to bring to our mothers. The cicadas provided sound effects each morning, signaling another hot, hot day, and the crickets practiced each early evening.

When we walked straight across the field, we'd get to a line of trees leading into the woods. The further back we went, the darker it got. Sometimes the only sound was the breeze high up in the oak leaf branches. Lightning had split a big cherry tree, and yet it kept growing with a gap in the middle of the split that became a tiny nature-made pond.

Every year we checked to see if a turtle lived in the pond.

"Hey Frankie, Mr. Turtle still here?"

We just knew with the certainty of our Miller Place childhood that it was the same turtle every year.

"Yeah, I saw him yesterday."

"You went back there by yourself?"

"Well, yeah, *I'm* not scared to go back there."

But he was. All the Squirts were.

There was one thin path straight through the woods and down a big gully, which led out to a paved road. As I got older, this paved road signified the dividing line between us, the pioneers of Miller Place, and the newer houses built up on the sand dunes. The newer houses had big sliding glass doors leading out to wooden decks and terraces where I imagined slender and tanned women sunbathed as their husbands or boyfriends took their boats out on the water below. This was the same Long Island Sound of our Woodhull Landing Beach, but it seemed more glamorous because each house had its own private beach.

◆   ◆   ◆

Off to the left at the back of the field, there was an old wooden shack. As adventurous as we were, especially Frankie, we never went and looked in the windows. It seemed too dark, and there was a funny smell, like old mud and dead leaves after days of rain.

One afternoon during the kite summer when I was nine, we heard a baby cry as we cut through the back of the field. Finn and I snuck up closer to the abandoned shack. There was a family living in there! A very skinny woman with long, dark hair came out of the shack with a little boy. His dirty pink arms were wrapped around the mother's neck. His legs were hooked around her waist.

I wondered if I had done that with my mother. For some time I had been intrigued by mothers and their kids. I didn't remember being held by my mother. There were a few hugs and kisses, but when I thought about it, it seemed I was doing the kissing and hugging.

One night washing up the dinner dishes, my mother told about how when she fed my Finn and me as babies, she could just sit Eileen and prop her bottle next to her.

"But you always had to be held," she reported as though this were extraordinary. Her tone of voice said this was a bother, but her smile told me she enjoyed it. Just another confusion about Mother. In my attempt to figure this out, I watched other mothers and sought out comparisons.

At the beach. "Mom, did you kiss the top of my head the way that lady just did to her baby?"

In the supermarket. "Mom, did I sit in the grocery basket and face you? Where did Eileen sit?" It was typical of my egocentric point of reference that I had no curiosity about where Ingrid was. She was just always around somewhere.

"Oh, stop that nonsense," was Mom's deflection. "You're too curious."

Curiosity with Mother was labeled a problem, but with Finn I could explore curiosity with great freedom. What would we find out about this family in the field?

"Jeez, she's so little," Finn whispered about the Shack Mother.

"And she looks so old. You think she's real?"

Just then two other kids came racing around the corner of the cabin. They stopped when they saw us as if there were a glass wall in front of them. We just stared at each other. Then we turned around and left.

We never told our parents about the Shack Family. It was like we knew they weren't supposed to be there, and if we didn't tell any grown-ups, the Shack Family would be safe.

One day, I was going to go back there by myself to talk to them, but I didn't even get close. From a safe spying distance I could see the shack was silent and empty. The sound of the goldenrod in the breeze changed from a soft swishing to a sharp clacking like a warning. *Maybe something bad happened back there.*

Before I even thought about it, my feet were backing away, then turning and running home. When I got home, my forehead and shirt collar were all wet from running all the way. I moved across the porch real fast.

"Eth—" Finn began.

"Gotta go," I stammered and went into the bathroom. My face looked extra skinny in the mirror and my eyes were wide. I was afraid. I didn't know what I was afraid of, and that made it scarier. I had that same feeling when Dad was late coming home from work, when Mom was frowning at me for being fresh, when Finn had fallen at Jenkins. But this was a new fear. A fear with no name. What does a nine-year-old do with that?

◆   ◆   ◆

That was the same summer the old car was abandoned at the other end of the tree line, farthest away from the Shack Family.

It was a blue and white Ford with rusty springs where part of the front seat had been ripped away. The turquoise leather back seat was all dirty and worn. For weeks, we went and sat in it each day, taking turns being the driver. It always sent us into crazy laughter when Frankie "drove." He tried to reach around to put his arm up along the back metal frame of the front seat as he turned to us.

He made his voice get as deep as he could, but it always squeaked out, "Where to, girls?"

Then one day, soon after the Shack Family disappeared, we found our taxi had been destroyed. The car seats were all slashed and the windows broken.

"Somebody must have been really mad," Frankie said. "Look at that brown paint all over the front seat."

"Why would anyone do that?" I wondered out loud. At first I felt confused. This was the first time I had seen intentional destruction. Then those small trickles of the unknown fear poked at the back of my neck. Even Miller Place had "dark" places. I didn't say so, but I felt afraid of the power of whoever or whatever could do that.

"Let's go," said Honey. We started to walk away. Our walking got faster until we were almost running. None of us spoke as if our silence would protect us from the danger we felt. We didn't go back to the car after that. I only felt safe when I walked through the field with Hank or Ingrid, and then it was okay to hold Ingrid's hand.

◆   ◆   ◆

That was also the summer the big kids played softball in the field almost every evening before it got dark. The softball field was another lawnmower-cleared area, courtesy of Dad and Mr. Jenkins. We could hear the big kids' voices as we hid in the goldenrod.

"Whoa, Starr's up. Move in. Move in."

"Yeah, just wait, Buster," came Starr's retort.

"OOOOh," a chorus of all the boys as they moved infield. Starr was pretty but she couldn't hit.

Our Squirts' game was to sneak through the shoulder-high weeds all around the field without any of the big kids seeing us. If we could get from the road to behind first base, second, and third, and then back out through the weeds to the road, we had our own home run.

"You go, Frankie. You're the littlest."

There was something exciting about crouching in the bushes as Frankie crept unseen behind first, then crawled his way to second base where the goldenrod was only waist high.

"Stop laughing. They'll hear you."

I couldn't hold back my excited giggles, especially when Frankie came back defeated because beautiful Starr had heard his famous monkey laugh and shouted, "Frankie, get lost!"

◆   ◆   ◆

There was a special part of the field that was off limits to the big kids. Finn, Honey, Frankie, and I took shovels and spades up the hill beyond where the houses were. We went way back into the field. It was like we knew we needed our own private place. It was ours by default, because it was the least desirable place in the whole field, the most overgrown with weeds and prickly vines.

This became our site for The Fort. We had seen the sign at our beach, a wooden painted sign that read:

WOODHULL LANDING BEACH—PRIVATE—MEMBERS ONLY

We made a cardboard sign like that:

THE FORT—PRIVATE—SQUIRTS ONLY

This was one place I knew would respect privacy. At home, everything was communal. I knew I had my own toothbrush and doll, but everything else was shared with my Finn and big sister—clothes, bed, toys, and books.

The year I was making my confirmation at our Presbyterian church, my mother was pleased with my seeming religious zeal. My zeal was really fueled by having my very own Bible. More important to me was the promise of my very own *new*, white confirmation dress. It was hard to enjoy the dress, however, when there was only enough money to get one dress, and my Finn was so unhappy wearing the hand-me-down, out-of-fashion dress that Ingrid had worn for her confirmation.

It was only when we were adults that Finn talked aloud of a more equitable, economical solution. "Why hadn't Mom gotten two less expensive new dresses instead of the one pretty dress for you?"

Why indeed?

Back to privacy. To be out in the field, away from grown-ups, moving the dirt, and controlling our space was worth any amount of work. We pulled weeds out until we had a shape about ten feet square. This was the main room of the fort. We used Grandpa's garden trowel and Mr. Jenkin's heavy metal shovel to dig. We dug down about two feet and piled the dirt up on the side for the walls. It wasn't hard because the dirt was so sandy. In a move of huge ambition, we each brought a gallon jug of water from the outside faucet at Grandpa's to wet down the dirt and pack it in hard on the walls. We lugged the biggest rocks we could find in the field into the fort room for our chairs.

"Oh, it looks great," breathed Finn.

Encouraged by our success, we dug yet another smaller room.

"What for?" asked Frankie, who was ready to play.

Having practical ideas, Honey answered sharply, "For the food room, dummy. We can bring sandwiches here and pretend this is where we live."

We worked every day until the weekend to get The Fort finished. That Saturday, the Squirts had their first of many private picnic lunches—sandwiches globbed with peanut butter and jelly and downed with root beer soda provided by Honey and Frankie, leaving the little milk cartons my mother had packed spilled out on the ground. I had a great sense of being safe when we all ducked down on the floor of the fort as a car drove by on the dirt road. No big kids, no parents, no chores. Just us. Just the way we liked it.

Although we always called it The Fort, the only enemy battle was when we indulged Frankie in his fantasy of being an entire tribe of attacking Indians and screamed him away.

With Our Hero

Chapter Thirteen:

Dad and Carol

My dad was always the coolest person. He was handsome and friendly to everyone. Every Saturday, he went up and down the beach talking to all the families. He shook hands with other dads and slapped them on their shoulder. Everybody would get the big Erickson smile.

I knew my friends envied me. He was always ready to flip us kids in the water. Other kids said, "Your dad is so *neat.*"

When we had the Fourth of July games at the beach, he was right there with the other dads and boys for the watermelon contest. A huge greased watermelon was put in a motorboat and taken out almost to Dead Man's Rock. Two men lifted the green greased treasure up and heaved it overboard. Boys and dads lined up at the shore. Mr. Jaasman, who took care of the beach property, stood on the beach and blew his whistle. The men and boys all dove into the water. The usually calm Long Island Sound was churned up with about forty arms and legs cutting and kicking in the water.

Racers swam out as fast as they could and dove down to find the watermelon. Then the fight was on to push, lift, and propel it to shore. Whoever was holding it when he swam in to where he could stand and lift it up over his head was the winner.

From other summer contests, my sisters and I had gotten used to Dad grinning as he held up the prize. The summer Finn and I were seven was no different. The boys dropped out, too tired to swim and grab at the watermelon, which was really slippery and would sink to the bottom. Others couldn't hold their breath long enough to dive down and begin the lift to the top. Soon only five dads were moving closer to the shore. The watchers edged in the water up to their ankles. I saw my dad right in the middle of the splashing. Then only four dads were left.

Who had it? Suddenly there was a dark shadow swimming underwater so close to shore. A head broke the surface, mouth wide open to take a gulp of air.

Daddy!

He was standing up. The water was up to his neck. He started walking in, then lifted the watermelon with his arms straight up over his head. Up the beach he came and dropped the watermelon on my mom's beach blanket. It was huge.

"We'll have this tonight at the cookout."

Weekend at the Beach

Everybody was in a good mood. Grown-ups and kids came around to shake his hand. Even the usually serious Mr. Jaasman was grinning.

"Your dad sure is a good swimmer."

"He was underwater all the way in to shore."

I felt warm from more than the afternoon sun. Dad patted my head as I reached up to hold his other hand. *This must be how proud feels.*

◆   ◆   ◆

On a Saturday in late August 1954, when I was only seven, my father was promoted from cool to heroic proportions.

We couldn't go to the beach because it was raining. Regular sun showers meant walks out on the road and jumping in puddles still warm from the sun.

This morning's rain was different, however. The windows in our bedroom were shut. The air felt chilly, but my bangs were sticking to my forehead. My bare feet felt sticky on the wooden floor as I walked out into the living room. All the windows in the house were shut.

"Mom, what's going on?"

The screened porch where we usually ate our breakfast was closed off. The wooden blinds along the screened walls of the porch were all the way down. Their drawstrings were tied to little hooks sticking up along the edge of the porch linoleum.

Dad had the small radio on the kitchen counter tuned to the news station. I could hear the weatherman talking through the crackle of static about a girl named Carol who sounded really strong and very mean. "She's ripped the shingles off roofs in three towns."

Mom poked her head out of the kitchen. "Get dressed." Her head went back in the kitchen. Something about her voice led me not to get dressed but to go into the kitchen.

"Get dressed," she repeated in that same flat voice. "Now. Go into the living room."

Finn and I shrugged and got on our jeans and T-shirts. No pretend games making the bed today.

Ingrid was already sitting on the sofa in the living room. She was sitting with her legs crossed and hands folded like she was in church. *Nobody ever sat on the sofa. What was going on?*

"But, Mom, what about breakfast on the porch?"

"I'll bring you some cereal and juice inside. Hurry. Hurry. Sit here."

She had the card table set up in the middle of the room with three chairs around it. Dad was in the kitchen making toast and coffee. My mother's movements were jumpy and hurried as she clattered bowls on the counter.

In response, my dad's movements were slower and more fluid. "Take it easy, Gladys," I heard him say.

I had been so surprised by this change of routine and my mother's nervousness next to my father's calmness, all I had been doing was staring at them. Now my other senses woke up. I could smell coffee and sweet, toasted cinnamon raisin bread. The snap of a wooden match on the matchbox. The whiff of smoke as Dad lit up a Camel cigarette.

Then I heard it: a steady rising sound outside, on the roof, and around every wall. Wind rising from a low, long swooshing sound to a deep groan that built to an awful high-pitched screech that rattled the glass windows and thumped the shutters against their hooks.

This was Carol. A hurricane. Hurricane Carol.

The rain hit the windows like someone was outside throwing buckets of water at the house. After the screech, the wind seemed to stop. I got up from our temporary breakfast table to move the few feet to look through the doorway and out our bedroom window. The metal glider that took both Finn and me to move just one inch was lying on its side, defeated by this wind.

The sound started up again. If the wind was a monster, it was stomping from the top of the driveway straight down at the house and around the bedrooms, and down the front hill, only to be followed by an equally ferocious and unfriendly mate. Thunder boomed loud. Too loud.

We heard a terrific *Cccrrrack!* out in the woods followed by a sound like tons of sand being poured through the trees.

"Tree coming down," said Dad. "Stay here in the living room."

The monster winds began their race again with our house right in the middle of their path. They either had to go around the house or through it. *Cccrrrack!* The pouring sand sound was closer this time, slamming on the roof over our bedroom.

"No! No! No!" My mother's hands were cold and clammy as she pushed us under the card table. She spread her arms protectively over the top.

That my mother was nervous was not anything new, but realizing that she was nervous *and* fierce at the same time was. Then and there I gave my mother the Finnish label I had heard my dad say once: *Sisu.* Fortitude. I usually reserved it for strong men or knights. But my mother showed *Sisu* then and all that day. It helped me feel a little less afraid, but I still thought the roof could crash and open us to the weirdly dark, daytime sky.

After our breakfast, Dad did something so very cool. He got out a deck of cards and sat on a chair by our table. I could see his pants and brown moccasins right there in front of me as I sat on the cold floor. He started thumping out cards on the table.

He's gonna play Solitaire now?

He dealt out five cards for each of us and passed the packs down under the table.

"Ingrid," he asked my older sister, "do you have any fives? Ingrid!"

"Uh, go fish."

The monster winds were still out there, but they weren't the center of attention any more.

We were.

Front View of Our House

Later that morning, the wind died down, and then stopped completely. The rain became a drizzle and then, wonder of wonders, the sun came out.

"Hooray, it's over."

We crawled out from our card table shelter. It was so still after the hours of that frightening wind. We just stood there looking out the front window.

Wet leaves stuck to the screen. Branches blanketed the usually cleanly raked hill. A huge tree was right across the steps leading down the hill, its roots sticking up out of the ground like a grotesque monster. When Dad opened the big front door to look down onto the road, we heard the weirdest thing.

Someone was whistling. *"May I go a-wandering ... "*

My sisters, mother and father, and I filled up the doorway crowding to see who this could be.

"Beneath the clear, blue sky."

"The hurricane isn't over," said Dad. "It's just the eye of the storm. The center of the storm is calm, but when it passes over, we'll be in for it again."

"My knapsack on my back."

A lone man in a green poncho raincoat appeared around the curve in the road. He was the whistler in the eye of the hurricane. Along the road in front of our house, and down the hill toward the beach he walked. We watched from the doorway until he disappeared around the bend going down Woodhull Landing Road. Mom kept the door open until we couldn't hear his hurricane whistle.

Dad decided if someone could venture out in the "eye," this was a good time for him to go outside and get the tree branch off the roof over the bedroom.

To the accompaniment of my mother's, "Allan, it's too dangerous," he got the ladder out of the shed and climbed up on the roof. Finn and I pushed open the bedroom window. The air was cool and clean like everything outside had been washed. We pressed our noses against the screen looking up to see just a bit of Dad's pants and shoes on the roof. He sawed at the branch until we saw it fall past the bedroom window. It thudded with a loud CLUNK! on the soggy ground. When Dad came inside, he went back to his coffee cup as if he had just taken a short stroll!

The eye passed, and after about a half hour, Hurricane Carol returned. Back under the hurricane table.

"Dad, why do they call a hurricane a girl's name?" This from Ingrid.

"Has there ever been an Ingrid, or Eileen, or Ethel?" This from Finn.

I couldn't resist. "Or a Gladys?"

Dad was sitting on the couch so I could see him smile at me and look at Mom. "A girl's name? That's just the way it is."

Mom stopped rinsing the lunch dishes and the water dripped off her hands as she held them just above the sink.

"But," he continued, "I never heard of a Gladys hurricane." He smiled over at my mom.

Mom gave him one of her quick smiles before she dipped her hands back to her kitchen chore.

We had dinner under the card table. There were more cracks of falling trees, but not as loud and not as close. I knew between the strong roof of the Miller Place house, my mother's protective *Sisu*, and my father's calm, nobody would get hurt.

And nobody did.

Chapter Fourteen:

Grandpa's Gardens

Picture this: my Grandpa Berberich as I remember him. I knew he was my mother's father, but to me he was "The Gardener." Every morning when I went out to the porch to eat my Rice Krispies, there he was, up the driveway by his gardens.

He was always slender, but as he got older he started shrinking. So he was stooped over in his shoulders and back. I don't think he was very old, but he was smart. We knew he was smart his whole life, which was why my Mother was smart too—that, and she went to college.

Grandpa had been married to my Red-Ribbon Grandma, but she died. He was the water superintendent at some big company and was quick with adding numbers and money, but that was when I was really little.

After he married Emma, he retired and became "The Gardener." He roamed his grounds, the gardens, walking the grassy lawn, stopping and looking at the trees, and touching the young raspberry and strawberry vines like they were really fragile.

He wore glasses with dark frames as he walked the driveway by the gardens. I guess they magnified things because his eyes looked big and kind of startled, like we had just jumped in front of him and shouted, "Boo." We would never do something like that because he was not that kind of a grandpa. He was not a jolly grandfather like my friend Nancy's grandfather, who was always laughing and sweeping her into a hug with big strong arms. Sometimes my grandpa teased Finn and me. "Ist dis der tvinsies?" he'd ask in a funny mix of German and English.

This was a problem. I didn't know German. I didn't know what I was supposed to say back to him.

One time I said, "Yah," and he drew his eyebrows together and his magnified eyes looked really scary. "Is der twinnie beingk Miz Smarty Pants?"

So we decided to say nothing after that. We just laughed and ran away and watched him from the shelter of the outhouse.

Grandpa seemed to have a closeness with nature that he did not have with people. His property was a haven for birds. Catbirds, wrens, robins, blue jays, cardinals, sparrows; we heard their calls early morning and evening. Little painted birdhouses were nailed to trees all over the acre.

The bird appreciation did not extend to other critters, like cats or moles or rabbits. The moles made long, thin mounds of tunneled-up ground that marred the smoothness of the grass.

Grandpa had established a "Dollar Deal" to discourage moles. Our job was to step down and flatten the tunnels to discourage the moles from living on our acre. He promised us a dollar if we ever actually trapped a mole. Even though a dollar was a huge amount of money when ice cream pops cost fifteen cents, it was enough of an adventure for me and Finn to just hop along on top of the tunnels.

"Think we're over their living room?"

"It's a mole world earthquake!" We'd stamp with both feet on the tunnel.

◆   ◆   ◆

One summer a stray, black cat hung around the house.

"Ssst. Get. Get out of here," my grandfather shouted, flapping his arms up and down.

"Oh, Dad," my mother said, "It's just a kitten. Leave it."

Grandpa knew what was important to him. "It'll kill the birds."

It did. But, instead of the cat getting chased away from our house, a saucer of milk appeared by the stoop outside our porch, a silent rebuttal to Grandpa by my mother. So we had a Summer Cat. Summer Cat was an outside cat. She was black with random white spots and white whiskers. She brought animal offerings to the bottom step of the house in homage to her benefactor, my mother: a small mole one morning, a little wren another day.

Mom whisked away the birds, but proclaimed loudly over the moles to my Grandfather.

"See, Dad, cats are useful."

How interesting!

I saw Mom put the saucer of milk out on the brick walk by our stoop, then sit down on the step and call in a low voice, "Here, kitty, kitty, kitty." In a minute, the little black cat slid out from the woods.

Then, the rough edges that always seemed to be around my mother smoothed away. It was like she was a sleepwalker. Mom extended her hand, just a little bit at a time, fingers moving together like she was rubbing a piece of silk. "Ch-ch-ch-ch-ch."

The cat tiptoed over and rubbed its head around her hand. Mom kind of hummed as her fingers scratched Summer Cat. She moved her hand away in slow motion and touched the saucer, and Summer Cat would go get her milk.

Mom never had conversations with the cat like I heard Mr. Kooney have with his dog.

"How're ya doin', boy? How's my boy?"

Mom just sat, keeping her eyes only on Summer Cat until it finished drinking, moved away, and began to wash its face with one white paw. Then it was like Mom moved out of her dream and stood up with a burst of energy. This made Summer Cat run off into the woods and Mom went into the house.

There were times in my childhood when my mother got impatient with me for "dawdling," or I'd see that uncomfortable pacing when she had money worries. I wanted to say, "Go into your Summer Cat dream. You'll feel better." But I never did.

◆   ◆   ◆

Finns at the Swing

All the Miller Place kids had another garden job: to keep the rabbits away from Grandpa's flowers. This was a dilemma for me because those little rabbits were so cute. Finn and I liked see how close we could get before they ran away.

"Oooh, cute bunnies." Finn pointed at the driveway.

"Shh, go really slow, so it hardly looks like you're moving,"

When we got closer, four brown bunny bodies froze, longish ears sticking up. We knew they were staring at us even though they didn't turn their little heads to look. I could see their noses actually twitch.

"They're like Flopsy, Mopsy, Cotton-tail, and Peter in the book," Finn whispered.

"Oh no! That makes Grandpa the mean Mr. McGregor!" burst out of me.

The rabbits were off in a mixed-up flurry of legs all in different directions.

Being good garden guardians, Finn and I shouted and halfheartedly tossed small crabapples at the rabbits. We knew we could never even reach them, so that covered all the bases.

◆   ◆   ◆

One night, just after supper, Finn and I had moved from the swing and were sitting on the glider on either side of my step cousin Hank. He had his arms up along the back of the glider, and we were nestled in so close to his chest I could feel his heart beating. His feet pushed on the ground so we were rocking back and forth. Ingrid had just got a good pump going on the swing.

"Rabbits in the garden," Ingrid called out.

Hank stood up, bent down like he was in slow motion, and picked up two small bumpy crabapples. His right arm came up fast. Where my aim and toss were short range, and my throw was kind of a lob rather than a fling, Hank's had force and speed.

Whoosh! The toss. The first apple bounced on the grass as the rabbit nibbled on a choice purple petunia. The apple landed pretty close.

"Whoa, you almost got 'im," Finn and I chorused.

The rabbit zigzagged off and away from the garden. The follow-up apple was sent to ensure rabbit distance from garden, but the little creature zigged when he should have zagged and apple met bunny on its downward arc. The rabbit gave a hop, but not a thumpity-thump one. It was more like a jerky hop, and then he clunked to the ground.

The glider stopped gliding. The swing stopped swinging. Hank's face was all white as he ran up to the grass.

The rabbit was dead.

This meant our Prince Hank, with his beautiful white teeth grin and his twinkly eyes, was a rabbit killer. We all knew Hank would never have really tried to hurt the rabbit. He just wanted to scare it away.

Who picked it up? How did we get it off the ground? I can't remember. The four of us needed to stay together that night, and it helped.

"I'll get the shoebox from Dad's moccasins," said Ingrid as she ran for the house.

"Don't tell." Hank's voice, almost a whisper. We didn't tell a grown-up till days later.

Eileen and I kept our eyes down on the bunny, so soft and formless, looking like his bones had all but disappeared with his last breath.

Ingrid's returning footsteps. "Here, put him in this."

We clumped together as one from garden to shed, Ingrid holding the box. Hank got one of Grandpa's smaller shovels from the toolbox. Back over to the grassy patch.

"Here. Right by the silver globe," Eileen pointed.

"Ooh, you think we should?" from the rule follower.

"Yes, yes." Some small relief in Hank's voice. "This is just right."

Hank speared the shovel into the garden and pushed the sole of his sneaker on top to push it down in the ground. One, two, three shovelfuls of dirt over to the side Ingrid put the box down in the dirt.

"Ashes to ashes, dust to dust," Eileen and I said in unison.

So, the bunny was buried in a place of honor by a large ornamental silver globe. We were all the same for that night. Ingrid wasn't the bossy older sister. Hank wasn't the shining handsome Prince; he didn't even go over to see Starr that night. Eileen and I weren't the little Squirts. We just were sad kids, all of us holding a tightness in our hearts.

The impromptu funeral procession moved back to the shed, the metal of the shovel making clanking sounds over the pebbles in the yard.

This was one death we kids were all in on.

Chapter Fifteen:

It Goes Without Saying

Once we settled in at the house in Miller Place, that acre of property, the field, the dirt road, and our neighbors defined the boundaries of our summer world. Sometimes, we walked to the Post Office to get the mail from our tiny cubbyhole box. On Saturday mornings, Mom drove to the General Store to get groceries or to the vegetable stand for Sunday corn. Poison Ivy Lane was the umbilical cord that kept us connected from the beach to the house. Most days ambled predictably and beautifully one after another.

It was a big event when our family piled in the car and drove into the harbor town of Port Jefferson. Today Port Jefferson is a shore town, a kaleidoscope of colors, mixing boutiques, bars, cars, boaters, and tourists. My childhood Port Jeff was famous on Long Island for providing the harbor for cars to ferry across the Long Island Sound to Bridgeport, Connecticut. On a clear day, we could see the tiny, hazy outline of buildings over in Connecticut. The thought of a big ferry going out into the Sound made me imagine a trip that probably took hours and hours and seemed a million miles away. For a ten-year-old, our Miller Place world was just the right size.

When we were in Port, Finn and I walked on either side of Dad, each of us holding one of his strong, warm hands. Ingrid and Mom were arm-in-arm behind us as we looked at fancy yachts docked along the wooden boardwalk.

"Look at that one. That's a beauty," Dad said as he paused in front of a shiny, wood-waxed Chris Craft.

"Shh, they'll hear you," my mother replied.

Now why wouldn't you want someone to hear a compliment?

It seemed Mother not only believed in children being seen and not heard, but adults too, depending where they were and who would hear.

I liked being able to look down in the little windows of the boats. "Portholes," Dad said.

"Look, you can see into the kitchen."

"Galley," Dad again.

We looked at people sitting out on the back of their boats drinking out of tall glasses. The women ate cheese and cracker snacks off little trays. The men sat with their legs crossed as they leaned back on deck chairs. Sometimes they lifted a glass and said, "Evenin'." Bet *they* never sat hunched over a card table with piles of bills in front of them like my dad, deciding who wouldn't get paid this month.

It didn't occur to me that the boat owners' lives of leisure meant lots of chores to keep the boats so clean and shiny. Someone was doing the grocery shopping to get the food into those galleys and then onto the pretty food trays. I only saw the ease and luxury.

You must have to be really rich to own a boat.

Finn and I called out the boat names and towns painted across the stern of the boats to impress Dad with our reading—then on to a geography lesson.

"Look, that one says Montauk. Is that out by the lighthouse?"

"Yes, that's where they came from. It's the port of call," Dad continued his sailing lesson.

"Bridgeport. Look, this came from across the Sound."

"Freeport, New York. Hey, that's near your office, Dad."

"Miami? How do they get all the way up here from Florida?"

Dad's habit of nighttime reading paid off. "The big ones go up the Intercoastal Waterway to Carolina. Then, they navigate inland routes to New York. I'll show you on the map when we get home."

The other magnet that pulled us to Port Jefferson was Gramma's. If it weren't yet dark, we left the boardwalk and headed to this soda shop that was halfway up Main Street. A little bell tinkled when you pushed open the heavy metal and glass door. A ceiling fan, circling at medium speed, kept the whole place really cool. Everything about Gramma's said *shiny, glass, clean.* A huge mirrored wall reflected a long counter with red stools. Above the mirror were shelves with all kinds of stuffed animals: little yellow or pink bears, black-and-white kittens, bunnies the color of the pistachio ice cream.

We knew never to ask to get a toy animal.

"Your father's not made of money."

Some day I will have enough money to have my bed covered with stuffed animals.

In later years, high school friends never questioned my desire for that little stuffed bear or rabbit as a birthday present. My bed did start to fill with animals that moved with me to college and my first apartment. Years later, my husband lobbied for almost a year before I agreed to retire that early symbol of wealth—the menagerie of brightly colored stuffed animals—to the window shelf instead of on our bed.

Back in my childhood world, Ingrid, Finn, and I walked next to the glass cases at Gramma's, and looked down at the round ice cream containers of boring vanilla or pink strawberry.

"Mmmm, dark chocolate. I want that." I could feel my mouth watering.

Ingrid led the way, "Hey, here's a new one." She leaned over to read the little hand-printed label. "Chocolate chip!"

I elbowed her away. "Where? Let me see. I want that one."

"Wait, here's another new one. Butter pecan."

Of course, I wanted that one too.

If it was a really lucky Port Jeff trip, we could order an ice cream sundae known at Gramma's as a "frappe," pronounced, "frap." Part of me loved it because it seemed French. Part of me loved it because of the chocolate ice cream, thick chocolate sauce, whipped cream, and a cherry on top, served in a tall skinny glass with a spoon that had an extra long handle to get all the way down to the sauce that slid to the bottom. Maybe I could have my frappe with chocolate-chip ice cream.

All of this was usually more than my mother would ever condone because of the sugar, which would ruin our teeth. She must have been right about this, because every time I went to the dentist I had at least two cavities. This meant the awful drilling, the funny burnt smell of the drill on tooth, and the sleepy fading and faraway feeling when the dentist put the mask over my nose and told me to breath in that laughing gas.

Why do they call it laughing gas? I never laugh; it feels too weird.

Then his voice came from far up near the ceiling. "Open wiiiiide."

That was during the other part of my life, however. Now it was summer. The taste of that chocolate syrup dimmed the fear of the dentist until it was a barely visible speck in my mind.

We sat up on the red stools at Gramma's and ordered. Most of the time it was an ice-cream cone to take with us as we walked back to the car. If Mom let Dad convince her that this particular weekend was special, then we'd have the frappe sundae. We stayed perched on the stools, and I watched myself in the mirror.

Who is that skinny girl with the ponytail and red ribbon? Do other people think she is skinny? Do they know she is a fast runner? Can that boy at the end of the counter hold his breath underwater all the way out to the buoy like she can?

I knew all those questions were so obviously about me. The label of being self-ish had been firmly attached to me by the time I was seven. For years, it filled me with shame, as if my selfishness were a physical part of my body—never to be beautiful, yet never to be cut out of me. Looking back now, I see this as part of finding *me*, not us, not the Twins, but *me* as a separate person in a world filled with so many other separate people. All the people around Finn and me in my childhood were single—singletons. I never was a singleton, and yet I knew there had to be a separate person inside me. No wonder I loved *Wuthering Heights* so much. I knew what Catherine meant by her words of love and longing, "I am Heathcliff." Just like I often felt, "I am my Finn."

If I were ever to be a separate person, where would I ever find that closeness with friends, with a boyfriend, with a grown-up like I had with Finn? Yet, as sure as I was of my life connection with Finn, I knew whoever loved me back when I loved them, would love Finn too. That went without saying.

◆   ◆   ◆

Besides Port Jefferson, we also went to the Woodman's house. Mr. Woodman worked for my Grandfather.

"Mornin', Mr. B. What we got today?" he asked as he slid out of his old blue truck. He raked leaves and pushed them onto a big blanket that he folded up at the corners and lifted up over his shoulder. Then, he hauled it to the garbage pit like an overstuffed Santa's pack. Sometimes he cut big branches off trees. He didn't talk to us, only to my Grandfather.

One day, I heard Grandpa telling my mother about Mr. Woodman's family.

I had been curled up on the porch rocking chair reading *Trixie Belden and the Gatehouse Mystery* when I heard Mom's rising voice. My eyes just looked at the page while I listened. Adult conversations were always interesting, even when they were confusing. I just knew all the things I overheard would fall into place someday.

"Woodman's got a wife and family over in Miller Place."

Neat. Maybe more kids for us to play with.

But then Grandpa called them by a name we were told never, ever to say. In our family, it was the worst thing you could do to call someone by a "derogatory" name. Somehow that rule didn't apply to Grandpa. I had heard him call people names in anger or simply out of impatience.

I didn't get it. Mr. Woodman worked for Grandpa and did a good job. Why would Grandpa talk like that about him and his family?

Even at the age of nine, it flashed through my head, *For someone who is smart about adding numbers and planting flowers, Grandpa sure is dumb about people.* Then, I felt guilty as if I had said those words out loud. With the "no privacy policy" in Miller Place, maybe Grandpa could hear my thoughts too, but he was staring at my mother.

When he said the word, "nigger" I thought, "That's it. Mom will yell at him and then never, ever speak to him again."

But she just stopped and stared at him. Her face was as still as if it were frozen. No yelling. She didn't say a word. She turned, climbed up the steps, and went right by me without asking how far I got with Trixie.

A new kind of battle? Very confusing.

A day or two later, when Mom announced she was going to the Woodman's house, I didn't whine when she said Finn and I were to go with her. She put some boxes of our old clothes in the car.

"Hey, Mom, what are you doing with those clothes?"

"We're taking them to Mr. Woodman's children."

"Why?"

"They don't have enough money to buy any."

Now I knew shopping for clothes at my house was reserved for the beginning of school (a new dress for each of us), Easter (a new dress, shoes, *and* hat for each of us), and maybe a party dress at birthdays.

"Are we *poor*, Mom?"

"No, we just have to economize."

Now, here was the Woodman family with so little money that they didn't even buy at all? *They must be Really Poor.*

"Get in the car," was Mother's only introduction to this early life lesson.

Finn and I rode in the back seat. Maybe we'd get to play with the kids. Maybe they had a swing. We could all take turns. I had learned how to pump myself and knew how to push someone on the back of their fanny so they would swing forward, but not so hard that they'd slide off.

"Hey, this is the way to the vegetable stand. Do they live near that?"

Not only did they live near the stand, they lived smack in the middle of the vegetable field.

Mom drove up a long, straight dusty road toward a low brown building.

Wait a minute. This was where they live? This was like our little shed! They live in a shed?

Mr. Woodman came out and got the boxes. I heard him thank my mother. I saw some kids in the doorway, but there were no smiles, no "Hello, come in for juice and cookies," like at Mrs. Desmaisons' or the Jenkins' house.

Sometimes, I'd waved to people from the back seat of our station wagon, but my hand never even left my lap to wave to the Woodman kids. Not a word was said to me or Finn. No little hands waved from their doorway, but there was a definite silent and invisible circle drawn around them, and another around us—and those two circles were in different orbits.

That summer, we made a few more trips to the Woodman's with clothes and books. Sometimes, Mom went into their house with the boxes. We always stayed in the car. It was like Mom couldn't go against her father, but she could let people know she wasn't like him.

◆   ◆   ◆

I don't know if she planned it or not, but the next summer, Mom's campaign came closer to home. We usually had a city child from the Fresh Air Group come stay with us for a week. My mother had gone with Grandpa's car all the way to the Port Jefferson Railroad Station to pick up this little girl.

"Our city friend is coming today," I announced to my sisters in a loud, important voice. "I'm going to have the table set when Mom comes from Port. I'm putting the crystal bowl in the center of the table. It will be like a party."

Our city child that year was a little girl whose skin was dark as could be. Grandpa looked stunned when the little girl came up towards the porch steps with Mom. He put down the new watering hose by the outdoor faucet and stared.

I stopped setting the table, clutching the forks and spoons in my hands. I was afraid to look at my grandfather and couldn't bring my eyes up to see what my mother was doing. *Oh, please Grandpa, don't say that word.* I looked down. I watched from the porch as the water from the hose snaked in a thin stream past Grandpa's moccasins and in front of my mother.

A silence started to grow. I had to look up.

Grandpa smiled down at the little girl. His old gnarled hand reached out and touched the top of her head. She smiled up at him, but leaned in next to my mother's leg so her face was partly hidden in the folds of my mother's skirt. Grandpa looked at my mother. She looked back at him.

Neither of them moved. It reminded me of the way the Summer Cat froze and stared when it was getting ready to pounce on a lazy butterfly. They just looked at each other.

Grandpa tilted his head and looked at Mom as if she were a new plant he found growing in his garden that didn't come out of his tray of seedlings. Then, he turned off the faucet, moved the hose away from the steps, and walked up the driveway and back to his log cabin. My mother had won a war.

It was years later that I asked my mother about my grandfather's prejudice.

Her response was, "I would have done so many things differently."

"What do you mean?"

"With you and Eileen (Finn and I were no longer a unit), with my father, with your father's drinking. You just didn't talk about things then."

"But, Mom, didn't Grandpa know how prejudiced he was? He had awful names for just about every group of people."

Questions poured out of me. "How did you know where the Woodmans lived? Did Grandpa tell you? Wait, did he tell you they needed clothes?"

The answers had to be in her head, but all I got was a slow, sad look from my mother.

Some things are still not spoken of.

"I know, Mom. I know." My mother's integrity may not have been spoken, but her actions those summers stayed with me forever.

◆   ◆   ◆

Years later when I was in high school studying U.S. History: The Revolution—Post Civil War, my teacher told us about sharecroppers.

"No, they didn't own the property, but they could earn money living and working on someone else's farm. The freed slaves often did this. Many people still do this today," he lectured.

"Slaves had names like Blackman or Thompson, given to them by their masters and owners after taking away their birth names," he continued. "Or names that defined their place and their father's place or work on the slave-owner's plantation, like Houseman or Woodman."

Woodman? My head snapped up from doodling hearts and curlicues on my desk to look at my teacher's face.

As an aside, he told us how European surnames could also illustrate place or occupation.

Mix this information in with a blend of information of my father's story about our name. *Woodman? Erickson?*

"So, Dad," I asked flippantly that night at dinner, "was Grandpa Erickson named for 'son of Eric'?"

"No." His serious tone got my attention. "When my father came to New York from Finland through Canada, no one could pronounce *Hauta-aho.* The immigration people probably just said, 'Better to give him an American name. He's Finnish. How about Erick-son?'"

In the time it took to write those eight letters, my Grandpa Erickson was stripped of his heritage and my father was robbed of his ancestral pride, but hey, they were "Americanized." I felt a thin, thin connection with the Woodmans. I wanted to go back in time and say to them, "That happened to us. Someone took my father's father's name too. It's kind of like the same thing."

But it wasn't the same thing at all.

Little Kids—Ingrid at 6; Ethel and Eileen at 2

Chapter Sixteen:

Growing Up

Every summer we marked our height on the porch wall of the white house. The wall was etched with pencil lines and dates laddering their way up toward the ceiling. When that one wall got painted, the measuring section was left alone.

Dad measured the first official height at the beginning of each summer.

"OK, back against the wall. No cheating," he smiled down at me as I lifted my heels up just a bit.

I lowered my feet down and away from the mix of pipe tobacco and coffee aroma that surrounded him. Long after my dad stopped smoking a pipe, the smell of cherry tobacco brought back that porch wall scene.

An old wooden ruler grazed in across the top of my scalp. Dad's thick hand wrote across the top with the flat carpenter's pencil. Our height lines got labeled with ETH, EIL and ING and the date.

"All righty. Here's where you were last year. Here's where you are this year." He stepped back and gave a little nod with his head, lips together in a straight mouth smile.

"OK. OK. Who cares about last year's marking as long as this one is higher? And it is, right?" I just wanted to go forward, into being more grown-up, powerful, pretty—not some skinny, little kid.

Dad gave me a solemn look. "Oh yes, it is." He caught my eye for another quick nod before he turned to my sisters. "OK, who's next?"

Finn's line was usually right next to mine. Ingrid was always ahead of us. I didn't think about how tall I might grow, I just wanted to grow—up.

Looking back, my dad didn't compare either—me to Finn, or me to Ingrid. A small gesture of seeing me as a separate person in a world of people who saw me as part of "The Finns."

He called me "Etta-quette," a combination of "Eth" and my endless questions about stylish ways of doing things ever since I learned about etiquette.

"Is this right?" I'd ask as my fork wiggled with the effort of holding it *and* keeping my pinky out straight. "Salt and pepper stay together," I murmured as I passed them both to Dad at dinner.

"Thank you Etta-quette," he teased, but it was a teasing that did not make me feel embarrassed. It was his way of saying, "You are trying to be a grown-up."

The Finns at 8

I checked my height weekly. Sometimes twice a week.

"Ing, do it again. Were those lines right?"

"That's the second time this week. How silly can you be?"

I never tired of standing up, back straight against the white wall, no shoes allowed, while Ingrid, acting the part of Dad, put the wooden ruler straight out over my head and marked with a Ticonderoga pencil line.

I felt Ingrid's hand pressing down on my shoulder as my bare feet rose up off the floor.

"Ethel, stop cheating."

"I'm not."

"You are too."

"Am not."

"Jeez, Ethel."

Whoa! I got her to say "Jeez." That was almost like a curse word in our house, but better let her have the last word. I needed her for the measuring. I lowered my feet.

I was always stretching as high as I could to be taller. Maybe prettier and older would somehow come with that rising height.

The Finns at 10

I looked at my older sister as she stood several inches in front of me. She was much taller this summer; my eyes were just up past her chest. *Wow, she has breasts!*

Starr got breasts last summer. I wondered when I would get breasts. It would be great if you could just go into a little booth like the bathroom stall at the restaurant in Port and "get" them.

"I'd like two round breasts, please."

"Hey, here you go, young lady." Poof—breasts attached.

I reminded myself to see if Ing's bathing suit filled out like Starr's did and mine definitely did not.

It seemed my mother was always comparing us to Ingrid. "Ingrid got all As when she was in fourth grade." "Ingrid could play that piano piece by heart in two weeks." "Ingrid never answers me back."

But, she didn't compare anything physical. What about the breasts? Would I get mine at the same age as Ingrid? *Could we write that next to her height line, "This was the summer Ingrid grew an inch in height and got two breasts"?*

Right now, my older sister was close enough for me to feel her breath on my forehead, which I found oddly comforting. She was wearing pink lipstick. Her blue eyes seemed bluer with her suntanned face.

"Ing, why don't you wear mascara?"

"Why don't you stop being so nosy?"

The females in our family have thin eyelashes that make us look like surprised penguins. Even without the mascara Ingrid seemed to be getting kind of pretty. Her hair was sort of wavy now that the Toni home permanent had washed out the frizz.

I shut my eyes and sighed. "Boring."

But I squinted just a little bit to see the other details of her growing up. Her teeth were really white and straight now that her braces were off. I *almost* wished I could change places with her, but if I were Ingrid, I would have to leave my Finn. So that kept it at *almost.*

◆   ◆   ◆

My mother marked growing up in different ways. She called them "privileges." She tried to make it sound really special. I knew privileges were what we were *allowed to do.* But some of these privileges had to do with being *told to do* certain grownup chores.

"Now you are big enough to rake."

"Now you are old enough to fill the bird baths."

Growing Up

♦   ♦   ♦

Some privileges marked the beginning of how far we could go from home. Ingrid's breast summer was also the first summer my Finn and I were allowed to go to the beach by ourselves. Now that felt grown-up.

Well, it was sort of by ourselves. Mother was walking down Poison Ivy Lane ahead of us, the strap of her aluminum and green striped chair wobbling off her shoulder. I started walking slower like my idolized Mrs. Desmaisons. She always moved slowly, her hips kind of rolling from one side to the other.

"What the heck are you doing?" My Finn collided into me. "We'll never get there."

"Must zhoo always rush?" I asked in my sophisticated French voice. "You miss ze beauty around you."

Finn stopped and swirled her towel out, over her head, and around her shoulders so it draped like a cape.

"Well," she said and stepped regally through the dead leaves on the path. It was a moment of grown-up royalty.

I looked down at her feet and saw her dirty, holey sneakers. She really was just a little kid and so was I.

"Come on, Miss Princess Towel," I said, swinging my beach bag at her. "Let's go. I'll race you."

We had small matching cotton bags with a pull string for our beach valuables. Mine banged against my knee, reminding me it held a blue plastic comb and brush set that the Fuller Brush Man had left as a sample, two barrettes, fifteen cents, and a small compact mirror I had sneaked off Emma's dressing table. Did I want to win the race or save the mirror from breaking? I slowed down just enough to stop the banging.

This was our first grown-up trip at the beach because we were allowed to sit away from the cluster of moms who were always near the water. It was a time-honored tradition that little kids sat with moms, and the teenage kids could set up an encampment at the back of the beach near the sand dunes. This way they could disappear up into the sand dunes to "make out" while everyone else pretended not to notice.

Honey and Frankie were already sitting like a small island away from the moms, with their towels laid out halfway between the shoreline mom camp and the teenagers.

"Put your towel this way—straight out," instructed Eileen.

"Wait, wait. Let's put them at kind of on an angle, so we can look all around."

"Oh yeah, we can watch them and her." No one had to mention that "them" was the big kids and "her" was Mrs. Desmaisons.

We ended up in a square with open space in the middle for bags. We faced each other with our feet in the middle.

"Wow, Frankie, your feet are really big this year. Your toes are enormous."

"They help me climb trees."

The square was the same arrangement our mothers had, but being about thirty feet away from the home base made all the difference to us. Those thirty feet granted permission to talk, giggle, and playact like the big kids.

"Frankie, put Noxzema on my back," I ordered in an awkward attempt at feminine wiles.

"Do it yourself." Frankie was indifferent to being the boyfriend.

"Let's eat," he said, unwrapping his peanut butter and jelly sandwich. The end to his lunch was a series of loud belches he produced with exaggerated wiggles in and out of his stomach.

His burps were followed by "Ugh, you're disgusting," from Honey.

Poor Frankie. He looked so surprised. Last summer we had flopped on our backs in laughter at the smallest burp. Nobody told him the rules had been changed.

Honey combed and recombed her wavy hair. I rubbed Vaseline on my lips like lipstick.

We could run back to Mom if help was needed. As long as the weather was sunny, and there were no threatened arguments, we were free.

Chapter Seventeen:

The Farm Caper

Sitting on the porch steps, I had a full view of the flower gardens and up the drive. Looking left, I could see the rope swing and gliders. Looking right, was the dark woods over to Kooney's. A brave bunny was heading towards the garden. It was too perfect a day to get up and scare a rabbit away. It was so like my idea of how paradise must be that the sight of a group of kids slowly and reluctantly walking down toward the house just didn't fit. What made it a "what's-wrong-with-this-picture" from my *Busy Bee Magazine* was the police car edging right behind the kids, leaving a dust trail in its wake.

A police car coming down our driveway?

It looked huge!

"Mom!"

What was most unusual was that my older sister, Ingrid, was one of the reluctant walkers.

"Mommy!"

My step cousin, Hank, looked kind of sheepish with his shoulders all hunched up. Starr's eyes were squinted like little slits and her mouth was smaller and tighter than I had ever seen it. Defiant. Ingrid looked at Starr and then poked her head out and looked sideways at Hank, who looked straight down at the dirt driveway as if he needed to guide each sneakered foot with his eyes.

I could tell Ingrid was scared, but not as scared as I think she would have been if she were alone. The group was going for Musketeer bravado. There was something just a little bit different about the way my sister was standing. Like she was separate from our little Miller Place world.

This was going to be interesting.

A gray-uniformed policeman swung out of the car and walked up to my mother.

"Seems these youngsters have climbed the fence and gone into that farm field down the road to stock up on tomatoes and corn—without paying."

We knew tomatoes were prime material for target practice. Trees, property, and street signs all bore the brand of the smashed red circle and dried yellow seeds of teenage daredevils.

But stealing corn? Why?

Were they going to bring it to their mothers for supper? How would they explain where they got it? Mothers knew they had to give teenagers more freedom than us little kids, but that didn't stop them from knowing how much money they had and how they spent it. It sure hadn't gone toward buying ears of corn.

Well, the farmer yelled at the kids to stop. Of course, they took off. The farmer called the cops. The cop easily found six teenagers running up our dirt road and just herded them down the driveway.

Sometimes my mother could get so upset at some things I said. It scared and fascinated me when she said, "You'll be the death of me." Was I that powerful somewhere in me that my fresh mouth would make her break in two and die?

However, when the outside world threatened, she was the powerful one. She grew at least five inches taller. Her frame was molded of steel. Her dark eyes were round, brown stones staring at the policeman. She stood very straight as he told the story while the petty thieves huddled together kicking up little pockets of dust in the driveway. I saw Grandpa coming down the driveway from the log cabin.

It was a whole other world out at the end of Woodhull Landing Road. I had never been out there on my own. Now those worlds had collided. The farmer knew Grandpa from the Beach Club. Grandpa was red in the face and walked faster than I had ever seen him move. He was mad.

"Emma!" he shouted back to the house. "Come out here."

It was Finn who came out and we sat on the porch steps to watch.

"I wonder how big the farm was."

"Maybe the farmer had a dog and he sicced it on them."

"Yeah, and they had to run all the way through miles of corn."

Our imaginations took over, as they often did, as we worked together to fill in the gaps of the current situation.

"Maybe the farmer had a shotgun," Finn whispered.

Oooh, this was serious.

Now grownups huddled with the cop. The thieves clumped standing in a circle with a small show of bravery, awaiting their fate. Sonny D., the rebel of the group, puffed out his chest even more than usual and reached for bravery rein-forcements. He tilted his head and squinted his eyes at my mom, not at the cop, as he pulled his pack of Luckies out of the rolled-up sleeve of his T-shirt. He actually lit a cigarette and took a drag. His hand was as steady as a rock.

Hank had a small, crooked smile on his face, until Emma grabbed him by his shirt collar and hauled him off to the log cabin. Her voice was louder than when she sang hymns in the kitchen.

"What were you thinking? How could you—?" Her voice carried all the way back to our house.

Finn reached for my hand. We had never heard Emma yell.

Bravado faded. The other kids melted into the woods. Once the thieves were split, their power was crushed. Ingrid burst into tears. She was forbidden to be with "those kids ever again." Hank couldn't see Starr for a month!

Finn and I looked at each other in disbelief.

"Starr is really going to be punished," I breathed.

Finn looked down at her feet. "Her beauty cannot save her," she intoned. "Even her beauty can't save her from these 'dire consequences.'"

That was sadder than our own sister getting punished.

Hank and Ingrid had to go to the farmer's for a couple of mornings to clean his yard to pay for the smashed tomatoes. They hung around the gliders for sev-eral afternoons doing nothing, but we all knew "forever" can't really be forever. Then it's too much work for the grown-ups to oversee.

Finn and I continued our watch.

Whatever pulled Hank and Starr together made them break the "forbidden to see each other" rule. I saw them kissing in Poison Ivy Lane only a few days after the heist, and soon Starr was on the little side porch at night again, right where she belonged—sitting on Hank's lap.

◆   ◆   ◆

After the farm theft, my sister Ingrid became a quieter but more interesting person. She spent a lot of time reading. I started to watch her to see what I could learn from her.

I saw that she was strong. Grandpa let *her* use the power lawnmower. She knew how to pour the gasoline in the spout and pull and pull and pull on the starter until the motor rumbled, then growled into gear. She could push it all the way up the hill and down. As powerful as it was, it never got away from her.

On Sunday nights, Ingrid started going to a church group. One Saturday night a small white car rolled down the driveway, Ingrid left the house by herself, and rode away to a new friend's house for a Sweet Sixteen party. When she came home, it must have been really late, because Finn and I were already in bed. We could see her from our window as she got out of the white car. She looked kind of flushed and smiley. Then she was out of view. We crawled to the end of the double bed to get closer to our bedroom door.

The screen door made that squeaky, then clinky sound, as my older sister went onto the porch where my parents were reading.

"How was it?" My mom's voice.

"Oh, Mom it was—"

We strained to hear, but the door between the porch and living room closed, shutting out the lamplight and leaving Finn and me, completely and literally, in the dark. We heard muffled laughter from the porch—Mom, Dad, and Ingrid—all together, just like grown-ups.

It seems she didn't have to separate from our paradise. Her Miller Place world simply spread out past the acre. What was labeled "The Farm Incident" by the grown-ups became known to Finn and me as "Ingrid's One and Only Rebellion."

Mom on Her Trapeze

Chapter Eighteen:

Rules of Engagement

It was an August night, so still the leaves were completely motionless, even at the tops of the oak trees around the porch. It was past lightning-bug time. Time to be in the house, but not so late that we had to go to bed.

I was looking at a photo of my mother. She looked about sixteen and was hanging upside down from a trapeze that must have hung from the swing tree by the glider.

Mom liked trees too.

My Grandma Berberich

Another even older black-and-white photo showed my Grandma Berberich dragging a big pile of tree branches. I remember her as being big and safe. Her lap was like a warm, private sofa. Her whole body was my soft chair. She died when I was seven, but she was my Red-Ribbon Grandma. In that photo she looked big and strong.

Mom looked over my shoulder at Grandma's picture, "Your Grandpa and Grandma Berberich cleared the land and built two houses. Originally, one was for me and one for my brother, Alex. Your Aunt Pauline lent Grandpa the money to buy the property."

◆   ◆   ◆

My Grandma Berberich had it all planned out. Her children would grow up, get married, have families, and go to Miller Place each summer. As we got older, being all together in the big white house seemed too crowded. Grandpa and Grandma had one big bedroom built onto the white house for them. That one room was so big; it had six windows. I never saw a room with so many windows. That one room had as many windows as we had in our bedroom, Aunt Pauline's old bedroom, and our living room combined. Grandma's beautiful mirrored dressing table was at one end of the room where the afternoon sun cast rainbow prisms off her perfume bottles.

My mother, being a good girl, followed the Miller Place plan. Being the girl in the family, she stayed close to her mother. My Grandma Berberich sewed all our clothes, and cooked most of the Miller Place meals. Mom's brother, handsome Uncle Alex, married dark-haired, beautiful Aunt Terry. They had one child, Cousin Karen, who was the center of their lives.

Berberiches and Ericksons

History and plans were revised. Karen got cancer. That wasn't in the plan. Uncle Alex and Aunt Terry moved to California. It seemed to have something to do with Karen's cancer. We didn't talk with them anymore.

Why would you not talk to someone just because they got cancer?

Karen was sick most of her life until just before she turned twenty, which was when she died.

In my family it seemed like when someone died they were just gone. We didn't talk about them; at least no one talked to us kids about them. It was something grown-ups took care of. All the people who died "would be OK in heaven."

Mom and Dad taught us a lot of rules to follow. "Don't talk with your mouth full." "Elbows off the table." "Shake hands and say hello when you get introduced." "Say thank you." "No cursing."

We learned some rules by watching and deciding what to say or what not to say. Death was one of those situations where no one said anything about how to act. Karen died at twenty. Today, I am alarmed to hear of death at such a tender age. I feel shock, deep sadness, but then, death was kept at a far and mysterious distance. I figured death equaled Poof! Gone. Vanished.

When Grandma died and Aunt Pauline died, Ingrid, Finn and I didn't go to their funerals. They just died. Poof. Gone. And "don't think of it anymore." I hadn't seen Aunt Pauline that much after she went into the old people's home, so I gradually did forget about her. There wasn't a big empty place in me when she was gone. Her place got filled up with friends and more of Finn.

◆   ◆   ◆

But way back when Grandma died, there were changes. No more big, soft, but strong lap. That was strange not to see her or be able to touch her and have her lap to sit on. I still had Finn and she had me, so gradually my emptiness got filled up a bit more, and we learned to watch how things happened.

There were other reminders that Grandma wasn't there anymore.

Mom said, "She held this family together like it was supposed to be."

My grandfather drank a lot. One time his car caught on fire because he was drinking. How mysterious, and a little scary. I didn't get the cause and effect of that. I was kind of nervous riding in the car after that, like it would just burst into flames if there were a can of beer in the car. Maybe that's another reason why my mother didn't like to talk about drinking. It seemed bad things were connected with drinking. But we didn't talk about those things. At least no one talked to us kids about them.

◆   ◆   ◆

When Grandpa married Emma, that was another confusing event. Mom and Dad got all dressed up. Mom wore a beautiful satiny black-and-white dress that swished when she walked. She looked like she was going to a great party. Dad wore a dark suit.

Finn and I agreed, "They make a handsome couple."

Emma, the bride, didn't wear a long white dress. She wore a suit with a big flower corsage up near her shoulder and a hat that matched the suit.

"Why didn't she wear a bride's dress?" I asked.

When Mom gave a little laugh in answer, I echoed her laugh, but didn't see what was funny at all.

If I had been invited, I would have been so happy going to a wedding party, but Mom wasn't happy going to this wedding. Mom looked so pretty, but in the wedding-day photograph, her smile looked like someone had drawn it on her face. Maybe she didn't want anyone taking her mother's place. None of us kids were invited. I figured it was because it was kind of a death. Like the death of Grandma Berberich being the boss of Miller Place. But we didn't talk about it; at least no one talked to us kids about it. There was more watching and listening to grown-ups talk when they thought we were asleep.

All seven of us stayed in the white house when Grandpa and Emma were first married. Even though they used the big bedroom, the white house didn't seem so big then with Emma and Grandpa, Mom and Dad, and Ingrid, Eileen, and me all together. Were the grown-ups deciding who the boss would be?

Grandma's beautiful, mirrored dressing table and bottles became Emma's. Emma laid out her perfumes and lipsticks on that very table. Each evening, Mom's hurt was ripped open again as Emma used the room that was her mother's. I guessed it was like the way the Three Bears felt when Goldilocks ate their porridge, sat in their chairs, and slept in their beds. In my childish way, I tried to reclaim the family ownership by trespassing in her bedroom. Emma must have known I sat at the mirrored dressing table and pretended it was my castle room. I looked longingly out the windows, first one, then another, watching for my prince to come declare his eternal love for me.

But she never said a word.

◆   ◆   ◆

The house was too small to have any privacy. Mom and Dad slept in a double bed; Eileen and I slept in the other double bed in the same room. Ingrid and Great-Aunt Pauline slept in twin beds in another small bedroom. I was envious that Ingrid had her own bed, but not enough to pay the price to bunk with Aunt Pauline, who snored really loud. The payoff for Ingrid came when Aunt Pauline went into the old people's home. Then Ingrid had the room all to herself, until Mom and Dad decided they wanted it.

Being in the same bedroom with my mother and father opened a secret doorway into some of their night talk. Sometimes my dad talked about drinking after work during the week. I would hear my mother sigh. He had promised he wouldn't drink too much; she had heard this before. When he was in Miller Place, he didn't drink a lot. I figured it was the Miller Place power my mother had to make him stop. That power didn't work as good when we were at our winter, spring, and fall house during the rest of the year.

Sometimes on other summer nights, they would be whispering and I'd hear a little laugh from my mother like Dad had told her a great, funny secret. Dad would make a humming noise. Nobody told me, but I knew they were loving each other.

Soon after the big bedroom summer, no more renters came to the log cabin because Grandpa and Emma moved into it. The log cabin had given up waiting for Uncle Alex and his family. It was small and cozy for Grandpa and Emma. Always being interested in houses, I found excuses to wander in their living room, touching the cool stone fireplace, tracing the knotty pine walls inside in every room, peeking in their small bedroom and bath downstairs, and lying on the double bed in the loft upstairs. The narrow kitchen led out to the screened porch that had a slate stone floor. The floor was cool under my feet even on the very hottest of days when my arms and face felt sticky and hot. A tiny side porch was on the other side off the living room. Maybe I could live there in the summer. I could be Grandpa and Emma's only child and have my own room upstairs. It seemed like a solid little fortress.

No, I couldn't go without Finn.

After Grandpa and Emma started to live in the little log cabin, things seemed better between my mother and Emma. Also better for us. I thought it was because my mother was more comfortable being the boss during the week in "her house."

The white house was furnished with beautiful old oak tables and dressers and pretty wicker chairs on the porch. We used real, but chipped, china dishes for everyday, which made an interesting match with the old jelly jars we used for drinking glasses. The glass cabinet in the living room held the precious crystal bowls and little crystal salt bowls with tiny spoons for individual servings. I couldn't believe my mother trusted us to wash and clean her treasures.

◆   ◆   ◆

Neighbors taught us things too. We could get to our next-door neighbor's property by cutting through a narrow row of dark green pine trees. This led to the Bramenger's. They only came out to the country on weekends, and they didn't have any children. They also didn't have an indoor bathroom. What they did have was a little one-seater wooden outhouse past the house out in their woods surrounded by huge oak and maple trees. The very tallest climbing tree was at Bramenger's just behind the outhouse, its branches making a natural ladder up to skinnier and skinnier branches near the top.

One cloudy Sunday afternoon, Honey, Frankie, Eileen, and I were up in the tree. It was swaying like it was a huge sailing ship on an ocean of cool air. Sunday climbing on the Bramenger's property held an element of danger, since that's when they came out to use the house. We had to sneak onto the property and climb up without any talking or laughing.

"Shh. Freeze. Bramenger coming," signaled Frankie.

We froze where we were on the leafy branches. Mr. Bramenger walked out with his Sunday newspaper to use the outhouse.

Honey, Finn, and I signaled with wide eyes and raised eyebrows. *Quiet!* Just the idea of us knowing he was in there and him not knowing we were up where we were was an outstanding event.

After he had ambled back up the path to his house, Frankie let out one of his famous monkey laughs, a combination of hyena and screech. *Perfect!*

Kooney's house was through the woods on the other side of our house. Patty Kooney was the same age as Ingrid. There was a narrow footpath worn through the woods by the big kids' nightly treks from house to house until they all met up with each other. They usually ended up by our gliders for horseshoe matches, on Grandpa's little side porch for cards and kissing, or at Kooney's house. When they were at Patty Kooney's, we heard the Teddy Bears hit single blaring through the woods. "To know, know, know him, is to love, love, love him."

◆   ◆   ◆

The Mitchell's property turned out to hold another life lesson. Their property included the woods between the Kooney's house and ours. Mitchell's driveway was the next one down the dirt road after our property. Their big white house was near the dirt road, and the rest of their property stretched all the way through, like ours, down to Woodhull Landing Road. This was important to know for one of those rules we learned later.

Being neighbors meant we all said hello and used each other's phone or bathroom in emergencies. We didn't go into neighbors' houses much, because everyone practically lived on their screened-in porch or outside on metal gliders with canvas-covered stiff cushions. It was with the Jenkins, Bramengers, and Kooneys that Finn and I learned about being a neighbor. The Mitchells taught us what enemies were.

It was really just Mr. Mitchell, the villain, and my grandfather, who were arguing. But somehow if one person in the family was mad at someone, we all had to be. This meant we didn't have to say hello to the enemy, and we could say bad things about them without a grown-up saying, "That's not very nice."

This was very clear with neighbors, but it got tricky when someone in the family was mad at someone else in the family. Like Mom being angry about Emma, or Mom being angry at Dad. Then what could we do? Mostly we kept quiet, but my stomach never felt quiet then, and I wondered why no one shushed me for my heart would make loud, beating noises.

One day, I heard Grandpa going down the basement stairs, rumbling and muttering to himself in a way that was strange for him.

Finn gave the first report. "Grandpa's mad at Mr. Mitchell."

Talking about how we felt was not the usual thing in our family. So naturally I wanted proof.

"How do you know that?"

"Well, Mom actually said Grandpa was mad at Mr. Mitchell, because he told Grandpa to take the shed down."

"Take our shed down? What for?"

"That's what I wondered," said Finn. "Earlier this morning, Grandpa was down in the basement and then walking all around the little shed."

"Yeah, I heard him."

"I thought it was weird 'cause now that he and Emma live at the log cabin, we hardly ever see him. There's nothing in the shed that he would want since Hank doesn't come out to Miller Place anymore."

No one talked about Hank anymore either, other than the short form explanation, "He's too old and had to work." So Hank was also "gone."

"Yeah, and what would Grandpa want with any of our beach stuff?"

Finn rolled her eyes at the stupidity of my remark. "I heard him talking to Mom," Finn continued. "Mr. Mitchell wants to put up a fence along his property. Grandpa's shed goes out over the property line. So Grandpa was measuring and grumbling to see if that was right. I heard him say the d——word too."

"Uh-oh, that's bad." No one cursed out loud in our family. The worst my dad ever said was "Dang it." It was serious stuff if we heard that.

This was threatening, but I didn't know that word to match that feeling. Miller Place had always been so completely safe. The dark fear place in the field had never come near our property. Now it seemed someone could come right over and take part of it away.

"Grandpa swore he was going to keep the shed up. Mr. Mitchell said he had some kind of power with a deed that said he owned the land."

"Come on, let's go see."

My mother was out by the shed following her father around.

"Dad, why do they need a fence anyway? Nobody goes—"

Grandpa's voice was choppy and loud. "Something about stopping those kids from cutting through the woods to get from here over to Kooney's. I'll show him who stops who."

Finn and I looked at each other in silent bewilderment. We knew a fence wouldn't stop teen travel.

Mom tried again. "Dad—"

"He wants a fight, I'll give him a fight! He'll know what an enemy he has made because of this. An archenemy. Archenemy—that's what he is!"

But Mr. Mitchell was going to win this battle. I learned a deed was powerful.

So this was what an archenemy was. Nobody told me right out, but I knew. Grandpa's archenemy could make Grandpa do something he didn't want to do. Grandpa would be mad forever, and we had to act mad too. We didn't say hello to Mr. Mitchell when he was cutting branches in his woods by our house. We didn't wave to Mrs. Mitchell when she drove by us on the dirt road, her little head just sticking up over the steering wheel. We'd stop and stare at her car, but her eyes looked straight ahead.

My grandfather did take part of the shed down, cutting it in half by taking off the wall on Mitchell's property and leaving the foundation with the bathroom open like a doll house you could see into.

"Let him look at the shower and all our tools and towels. See how he likes that," was Grandpa's statement.

Mr. Mitchell's house was way down at the other end of the property by the log cabin. Where Grandpa's property was all groomed, gardened, grassed, and cut, Mr. Mitchell's long, narrow acre was scruffy woods. So, the only people who saw the ruin of the shed was us: a sad reminder of the days when Hank lived there; and he got cut away too.

When our big house was painted, so was the remaining side of the shed, but the cut side was left raw and rotting like a neglected sore.

◆   ◆   ◆

Some days, when we were almost at Poison Ivy Lane on the way to the beach we'd hear a screaming noise like a car horn that got stuck. We'd kind of smirk and go, "Oh, that's Eddie."

The Bobson's house was last on the dirt road and Eddie, their only child, was different—actually weird. He stayed by himself, didn't talk right, and was prime teasing material by younger, but more clever children.

Our mothers' warnings to "Leave Eddie alone" were open to interpretation. It could mean, "Be Christian" and be nice to him. Or, it could mean actually leave him all alone; isolate him. With no direct explanation, we tested our weak sense of power by teasing someone with even less power and then running away on our strong, tanned legs as he loped after us on strangely uncoordinated, pale ones.

We did not play with Eddie and pretended to be an exaggerated copy of him by deliberately drooling and slurring our words. The "pretend to be Eddie" was usually only short, crude imitations, but ones that were cruel, even in their brevity.

Eddie took over the Ford car in the field after we had abandoned it. He grew very big and tall as we all aged, but his mind and speech stayed at the level it was when we were really young. He also stayed alone. I was intrigued by Eddie and wanted to talk with him, but like going back into the field by myself, I wasn't brave enough, and I certainly wasn't going to break the family rules. I'd leave him alone.

A dozen years later, when I began teaching young children, I saw "Eddies" almost every year in my classroom. Eddie was the child no one wanted on their team, the one who was too gangly, too sloppily dressed, not smart enough, the one who got caught when all the other kids ran away from a prank. I think I tried to make amends by being kinder to that child, maybe even favoring him.

I'm sorry, Eddie.

Beach Bookends

Chapter Nineteen:

Mr. Jaasman's Woodhull Landing Beach

Every year since our Miller Place childhood, when Labor Day weekend has come and gone, I am forced to accept that summer is over. Summer, with its bewitching days filled with piercing noonday sun and late afternoon light filtering through an umbrella of tree leaves. Summer, with its evenings serenaded by the dwindling song of crickets. Memories of childhood summers spent swimming, diving off rocks, and feeling completely free at the Woodhull Landing Beach come flooding back.

In Miller Place, until the dreaded Labor Day, my twin and I were free as soon as our chores were done. We made our escape down Poison Ivy Lane, to inhabit the two acres of private beach that were host to mothers released from wintertime worries and kids let loose each day. The only reminder to go home for dinner was the sun sliding west toward its bed in the Long Island Sound.

My usually serious mother was more relaxed in those summers at the beach. At "home," our winter home, unpaid bills, or the broken hot water heater kept that worry line along her forehead, but not at the beach. There she was cocooned with the other mothers by the salty water's edge.

◆　　　◆　　　◆

Believe it or not, the highest authority at the beach was not my mother. The entire beach was ruled by a massive, tanned man by the name of Mr. George Jaasman. The fact that we never even thought of calling Mr. Jaasman "George" or "Mr. J" was a strong message of the power and respect he commanded. In all the years at Woodhull Landing Beach, he was always there, from morning to six o'clock in the evening. His work clothes consisted of long khaki pants, old scuffed brown leather shoes with no socks, a sleeveless undershirt, and a whistle on a long, skinny cord around his neck.

My grandfather, the ice cream man, Mr. Woodman, and Mr. Jaasman were the only grown men around in our summer community until the dads arrived on Fridays. Maybe that accounted for my fascination with him. He looked ancient when we were little kids and still looked the same when I was a teenager. *How did that happen?*

He was someone who seemed to live his life exactly the opposite of what I had been taught about grooming, manners, health, and strength. I watched him closely to try to figure him out. He looked kind of unkempt with a grizzled, grey beard. He wasn't really that polite but we had to be polite enough to say hello to him every day. Because he wasn't a friend and we had no social relationship with him, I knew I was allowed to stare at him, although with anyone else it would be rude.

Did he live alone? Was there a Mrs. Jaasman? Was she just as tan as he was? Was she as big as him?

He sat with a can of beer in a sagging beach chair under a faded umbrella by the driveway entrance to our beach. The chair sagged because Mr. Jaasman was the widest man I had seen in my entire life. He was a bit over six feet tall, but his pants were so big I thought two of my dad could fit in them. His brown belt disappeared under the belly that hung over his waist.

His arms were thick and muscled from his pudgy, calloused hands to above his elbows. But up above his biceps, his skin looked all saggy and wrinkled. Yet I had seen him lift up a huge railroad tie by himself as he opened the beach gate.

He never wore sunglasses, and I never saw him use any suntan lotion. His skin was such a dark coppery color from the sun we figured he probably stayed tan all year. Maybe he just went down to Florida in the winter and was the tyrant ruler over little kids on some other beach.

From his post, Mr. Jaasman checked badges and car stickers for the Woodhull Landing Beach Club: the WLBC.

AUG   55

Miller Place

On the Beach with Grandpa

My grandfather had started this beach club when my mother was a little girl. He and a group of summer vacationers bought the strip of land atop the dunes and the thousand-foot tract of beachfront. It never became more than a black-topped parking lot with two old spider-filled outhouses in the back. There was a wooden ramp some of the dads put together that went down the more sloping side of the sand dunes to the beach. Wire fences at either end marked off our area from the public beach to the right and the glamour beach to the left.

Mr. Jaasman nodded and said, "Hello," but without a smile as we filed in at the driveway.

"Badges?" he always asked.

We had been marching in and out of the beach driveway for our entire lives and we still got "Badges?"

"He's so mean," Frankie whispered from under the pile of round swimming tubes he wore in a column over his shoulders and piled up to the top of his head. We made fun of him for carrying them like that, but not too much because he carried all of our tubes too.

"Yeah, meanie, meanie, Mr. Jaasman," I whispered as I twisted the badge around my bathing suit strap. But I didn't really believe that. "Very stern" fit him better. He saved his smile for the moms who paraded by. They were like a daily Mrs. America Pageant. Instead of high heels, tight bathing suits, and empty hands with lacquered nails, our proud contestants wore espadrille sandals and skirted bathing suits and were loaded down with chairs, towels, beach bags, and picnic baskets.

Besides checking badges, Mr. Jaasman probably covered the legal requirement for a lifeguard. Occasionally, he walked to the top of the sand dunes, put his binoculars up to his eyes, and peered down at the water.

"Mr. Jaasman's doing his check," said Frankie from our outpost on the beach. "Same as usual. First he looks over to the rocks where the big kids are diving. Now he's looking out to Dead Man's Rock."

That got my attention. Everybody knew you had to be a teenager to swim to Dead Man's. I had been swimming and leaping off my father's shoulders since I was six and had no fear of water, but Dead Man's?

"I could swim that distance to Dead Man's," I bragged.

"Yeah right," said Honey, "The distance, sure, but DEAD MAN'S?"

I couldn't answer her. The power of that name—Dead Man's—kept us little kids in closer to shore. Maybe there really was a gray bloated body slung over the pointy rock on the far side like the big kids said.

"Well, I'm definitely going as soon as I'm thir-TEEN."

"Sure," Finn chimed in, "We'll all go out there together."

"Yeah." A chorus of agreement—action postponed for about four years.

Frankie continued his report, trying to make his voice sound like those radio announcers for the baseball games. "OK, his glasses are scanning the horizon."

"For what?" I questioned. "The water's always calm. The biggest thing out there might be a sixteen-foot motorboat. I think Mr. Jaasman was a sea captain who lost his ship because of a—a sinister scandal. He stole his neighbor's ship and got caught and this is his sentence. Never to go out to sea again."

We'd been through this story before. I could never decide if he was the villain or victim of an evil plot.

Maybe his search had less to do with protecting us and more to do with getting a closer view when the excited shout of "porpoises!" traveled like a verbal wave along the beach. As if "porpoise" were the cue, kids threw down sand pails, moms got up from low beach chairs, and teens untangled themselves from striped beach towels and ran to the shoreline. This was kind of funny because the beach wasn't that wide. I liked to be in the same water as the porpoises even if we were only along the edge, and they were out so far they looked like miniature, jumping fish. Moms and kids were all smiling and pointing. "Look. Ten, eleven, twelve of 'em."

When the fish had disappeared, the moms stayed at the shoreline, wading and talking with their arms crossed, doing little kicks at the water with their feet.

The Squirts became the porpoises, diving and jumping up out of the water until our eyes burned from the salt water.

Mr. Jaasman's other role was self-appointed moral barometer. After the horizon check, his head would dip down and back to the rear of the beach. His loud whistle then meant the big kids were fooling around in the back and not only kissing but also *lying down and very close to each other* on their towels. So *that's* how the sand dunes became so popular.

For us to be allowed to sit on our own was exciting, and yet we became another group for Mr. Jaasman to watch. A sharp blast on the whistle for us meant Frankie, or one of the other boys on the beach, was throwing sand at us.

The long blast came one day when Timmy, the skinny kid from the other end of the beach, came running over and poured a pail of water down my back.

"Hey, you, get away from the girls."

Poor Mr. Jaasman. He could no more stop boys from getting interested in girls than he could go out and swim with those porpoises. Years later, when I graduated to the back of the beach, I found out the excitement of kissing in the sand dunes.

"You twins are just like your Mama," was Mr. Jaasman's admonishment. "You think you kids invented all this?" He still sounded stern, but then I saw the twinkle in his eyes.

I had been rubbing Noxzema on my nose that day when Timmy poured that pail of water. Although I secretly wanted freckles on the tip of my nose like Starr, the act of applying Noxzema like make-up put me more in the class of Mrs. Desmaisons. I got a glimpse over my shoulder of Timmy's blond hair and big smile as he ran away, laughing.

Frankie's bucket of sand down my wet back made me answer "OK" to his, "Come on, Dopey. Let's go swimming."

The race to the water was accompanied by lots of yells and screeches. The stones never hurt our feet. The water was never too cold. That first taste of salt water was delicious.

It was almost like a beach rule to dive and swim as far we could underwater. I loved being in the water; I felt completely at home and buoyant. My hair streamed back, and my splotchy tan looked smoother underwater. Maybe I'd turn into a mermaid. I made myself come up slowly, kind of like Mrs. Desmaisons. I felt a sense of what might be called grace.

"Ethel, you ready to play?"

Turning quick back to my friends. "Yeah, yeah."

"One, two, three, go."

Jump up in the water, bend down into a squat, and sit cross-legged underwater. Cross your arms in front of you, then exhale, and talk. You could never tell what the other person was saying, but the bubbles coming out were beautiful.

"Ok, girls, get out now. You've been in long enough," came my mother's voice.

"What? We just got in."

"Out. Your lips are turning blue."

Turning to Finn, I could see her shivering and her lips were kind of blue. I knew my jaws felt tight and were quivering a little, but I would never admit that to Mother. What you didn't admit, just wasn't happening.

"Out now, and dry off."

"Oh, okay! Okay! Jeez." I never knew till I was a teenager that "Jeez" was like a disrespectful nickname for Jesus. That was worse than calling Mr. Jaasman "Mr. J." My mother strove for formality as a barrier to ward off future teenage rebellion.

"What was that, young lady?"

Those two words, "young lady," had all the power to remove any sense of independence. Quick as that, Mother closed the independence gap I had gained with my thirty feet of towel distance.

"You just sit over here by me until I tell you to get up."

Finn often got included in the consequences of what was known as my "quick mouth." She never complained either. We could be together and start a new fantasy game even if it was one of those "and not a word out of either of you" situations. I didn't mean to be bad, but thoughts came into my brain, traveled through the word chute right down my head, and out my mouth before I even was aware of it.

◆   ◆   ◆

Just when we thought it would be too, too hot to sit anymore, the most fantastic sound would be heard from the top of the sand dunes: small bells, yet heard on every beach.

"It's the ice cream man!"

"Mom? Mom!"

"Ok, go ahead." My mother's reprieve was delivered in a tight, serious voice, which couldn't dull the lure of an ice cream treat.

The ice cream man parked on Woodhull Landing Road at the top of the sand dunes several times a week and always on the weekends. Maybe he knew Weekend Dads were more open to buying ice cream than the Daily Moms. After all, dads worked all week, and being a spender on weekends was part of their reward and the offering to us for their absence.

Up the ramp we went, running on tiptoe over the burning black tar parking lot. The white ice cream truck always parked just outside the gate of our beach. Wiggly kids lined up by the back door of the truck like it was a refrigerator freezer, only complete with color pictures of the treasure inside.

"Where's my dime?"

"What are you going to get?"

"I don't know. I have to look at the pictures."

"Oh come on, you always get the same thing. If you have ten cents, you order Italian ice. If you have fifteen cents, you get Toasted Almond pop."

Toasted Almond, my favorite. Crisp semi-frozen vanilla ice cream rolled in crushed almond bits.

The ice cream man took several orders at once, opened the door, and leaned in until the top half of his body all but disappeared as he searched inside the frozen store. When he came out, a cloud of cold, white air swirled around him.

"Oooh," we all sighed.

"Here y'are, little lady."

"Quick, get the paper off. Come back here to the shady side of the truck so it won't melt so fast," Honey instructed.

"Mmmmm. I love Toasted Almond," Frankie said in between licks.

"You say that every time," Finn pointed out.

"Well, I love it every time," was his reply, which made perfect sense to me.

Toasted Almond popsicle came on two wooden sticks. The first bite, so cold it hurt your teeth, sent a little *zing* up inside your forehead. You had to bite off in the center between the sticks where it curved in to get it to break apart just right. One time, I ate mine too greedily any old way, and when I went to break it, the whole pop was on one stick. Over-burdened by too much ice cream on one side and the heat from the sun, it sagged before my eyes and dropped into the sand. Sweet, sweet ice cream. The paradox was wanting it to last, but not have it melt or drop.

Italian ice was another treat, like sherbet in a small Dixie cup with a wooden spoon that you used like a mixer, mushing it and squishing the spoon down into the ice until the fruit color and flavor stirred up to the top: dark raspberry, blueberry, or pale yellow lemon. I rotated ordering each until I was about ten. It was then I stopped ordering blueberry because I realized it turned my teeth a grayish blue. I began another attempt at acquiring beauty as I ordered only raspberry after I saw how that flavor turned Honey's lips red. It was the red of the small Berry Red lipstick on my mother's dresser, a small two-inch sample from the Avon lady I had been eyeing for my beach bag. That switch to raspberry Italian ice saved me from petty thievery.

Ice Cream!

Chapter Twenty:

Mermaid Lagoon

Being nine was easier than trying to be beautiful. After ice cream, we raced down the flat wooden ramp that led back to the beach.

"Let's go to Mermaid Lagoon." Who else but little kids would see a safe haven for mermaids in a large clump of seaweed-covered rocks down at a deserted beach?

Long Island Sound beaches are made up of rocks and pebbles and sand, but mostly rocks and pebbles. The really sandy part is only towards the back, as you get closer to the sand dunes. After the early summer days of hobbling over the sharp pebbles and larger rocks, and then weeks of walking on the stones, we were oblivious to the sharp edges of the rocks. We usually walked along the water's edge going to Mermaid Lagoon. Wet rocks always looked shinier. The wet Indian-red rocks could be scraped against each other and used as war paint, or for designs, depending on our game. Mermaid Lagoon called for painting curlicue lines up our arms, underlining our eyes, and putting circles of "rouge" on our cheeks.

Off we went, single file along the shoreline, with Frankie veering off to dive in the water and then doing kind of a hopping run up to his waist to keep up with us. Even with Frankie doing his hop swim in the water, it was a different mood when we went to the Mermaid Lagoon Beach. It was much calmer. Quieter.

On this particular still, sunny day, Honey was the leader. Finn and I filed behind her, stepping in her wet footprints so anyone trailing us would be tricked into thinking it was only one walker. The single set of footprints led to the end of our beach, around the fence and along the shoreline of the public beach, around another wire fence and across to, of all things, a convent beach.

"Don't you think it's a waste to have a convent for the nuns right on a beach?" I asked, but in a low voice in case the nuns or God could hear. "I bet they never race in the sand."

"And they never lie out in the sun," said Honey. "At least, we've never seen them do that," she added with kind of a giggle at the thought.

"Maybe they go swimming after everyone else goes home to dinner," suggested Finn.

"Maybe," We eyed the top of the dunes looking for some kind of sign of nun bathing suits. Nothing. No one.

After we passed the empty convent beach, there were no more people, no noise—just hot sun, flat pebbled beach and almost non-existent waves on the ripples of the incoming tide.

Mermaid Lagoon was a group of large rocks, covered with ugly, bumpy barnacles and skirted with lime green, slippery seaweed. Mermaid Lagoon was prime for visiting when the tide was not quite all the way in. If the tide was in, then the rocks were too far out into the water, and we were afraid to swim out by ourselves with no grown-ups around. If the tide was out, the rocks were totally exposed on the rocky beach and it was like a dry desert.

"Yowie," Frankie shouted. "The tide's coming in. It's gonna be just right!"

When we reached the two big clumps of rocks, the bright green seaweed was floating off the edges of the rocks in the water. With the waves swirling in around the Lagoon, there were small pools of saltwater trapped in the kid-sized crevasses.

Honey climbed up near the beach side to sit in the sun. Finn and I crawled into the sun-warmed water of a mermaid cove to wait for another wave. It swirled in around us, and we floated up in the salty water.

The sharp barnacles that protruded off the top of the rocks kept seagulls off, but that didn't stop us. After our mermaid bath, we sat up on the highest points of the rocks out of the water and pretended to brush our hair while Frankie swam around the rocks as our pet porpoise. In my mermaid play, my hair miraculously grew down over my shoulders and down my back. As the sun dried my hair, it felt heavy with salt, and I could see salt spot on my arms. Maybe this mermaid would have to get wet again.

"We better go back," Honey pointed. "The sun is going down behind the dunes."

On our walk back to our beach, Frankie suddenly stopped and held up his hand in a "halt" signal. He stretched his arm up toward the hill. Seven nuns were curving down the steep, narrow wooden stairs from the convent at the top of the sand dune.

"Think they're actually going in the water?" I whispered.

They looked completely dressed, with black-and-white habits covering their heads and long black bathing suits covering their legs. What was so interesting to me was that they were completely silent. How could you get near a beach and not want to jump and laugh and throw your arms up and out to the sun and water? The quiet was like a no trespassing sign. Their silence seeped into our air so our voices were stilled also. We started walking along the water's edge again, heads bowed, hands folded, like little praying mermaids. Peaceful, but strange because they probably tolerated us as mermaids. I bet if we had been noisy kids, they would have motioned us away with long pointed fingers coming up out of black sleeves.

"Frankie, don't look back," Honey said in a Mom-like voice and a pinch on his arm. "It would be like Lot's wife," she added with a twist to the biblical story.

Mermaids we were until we got back to the noise of kids shouting in the water at the public beach, where Frankie was freed to entertain us with a real full and juicy belch.

"Ugh, Frankie," Honey protested.

But Finn and I laughed, relieved to be back on familiar ground.

Chapter Twenty-One:

The Sunday Climbing Tree

Sundays were special. It was church day.

The summer I was eleven, I just wanted to stay home on Sundays and play in the crabapple tree by the driveway. About once a month, Finn and I were left behind and spent church time in that tree, and so we called it The Sunday Climbing Tree.

"Please, Mom, I had a bad dream last night. I'm so tired. Can't I just sleep a little this morning?"

"No. Get up." No arguing when Mom used so few words. Off to church.

Several Sundays after that Finn and I concocted a more elaborate plan.

"Tell Mom your stomach hurts and you have to sit in the bathroom too long to be ready for church," I urged my Finn who did like to spend time alone. Sometimes the bathroom was the only place to find that solitude.

"No, you tell her," Finn's muffled voice came from behind the closed door. She'd participate in the hoax but didn't want to be too upfront about it.

"Mom, Eileen is still in the bathroom, and I didn't even get in there yet. Can't we just stay home? We'll help Grandpa." Offering to do chores was sort of a shortcut to heaven, and to make the offer for Grandpa always held extra merit.

A sigh from my mother. "Oh, all right. But stay on the property."

All went according to plan. My grandfather gruffly allowed that we could stay with him while my mother, father, and older sister went to church. A chore exchange was involved.

"Take the dust brush and get all those cobwebs off the gliders." Grandpa tested me to see if I'd cringe at the thought of spider webs.

I grabbed the wooden brush from his hand and ran back into the house. Grandpa's acceptance of being the substitute parent usually ended as soon as my parents were out of sight, because so was he.

"Finn. Come out. It worked. We have to get the spider webs off the lawn chairs. Then we can go to the Sunday Climbing Tree."

The Sunday Climbing Tree—Heaven itself bordering the driveway, its branches cutting up into the sky above the peach, pear, and cherry trees. A small V nook way up near the top swayed with a delicious scariness on a breezy day. There was a limb extending out over the garden near the bottom. Finn and I both fit side by side on a great long branch that stretched out over the driveway.

Finn's digestion problem solved, we dusted off the furniture and ran up the driveway. We were at our driveway branch outpost about five minutes after my dad's blue station wagon had disappeared up the drive on the way to church.

"Let's stay up in the tree until they get back from church."

The Sunday Climbing Tree was most often a towering ship, the grass was our stormy sea, and the fallen apples other shipwrecked boats and passengers. It was easy to spend an hour in the tree, never touching ground. I rescued drowning passengers by hanging upside down by my knees on the garden limb. From there I scooped up one, two, or three grateful, crabapple survivors.

That Sunday, I climbed up to the tippy top to scout for pirates. It was easy going up.

Right hand on the knobby branch, left foot up, left hand reaches up to the branch, and pull up. I felt like I was on top of the world.

"Ahoy down there, scout," I called back to Finn. "Any sign of land? Looks like a storm a-brewing ahead. But we'll be safe here in the harbor."

This was better than church. I must be closer to heaven than anybody sitting on those hard pews.

When I looked down, I realized I *was* on top of the world, at least the highest my world had ever been. Too high. I felt like one of those statues in the Davis's cemetery up the road—turned to stone. My arms and hands clenched the branches. I knew I needed rescue.

"Finn! Eileen! I can't get down. I'm scared." I couldn't even turn my head to look at her. "Eileen. Help me!"

"I can't come up that high. I just can't. Hold on." She kept talking to me. "Just hold on." She sat on the tree limb way down below. "I am looking up at you. You look like you are OK."

My rescue ship appeared up over the rise in the driveway—a light blue ship that looked vaguely like our Rambler station wagon.

It was not a hearty "ship ahoy" that greeted the blue car on its return from church but my twin sending out an SOS for help. When you are eleven, the best hero is Dad, Pops, or in this instance, Daddy.

Rather than climb down and leave me, my Finn called and called.

"Daddy! Ethel's stuck. Daddy, come get her down."

"OK, I'm coming," came Dad's deep, even voice.

I heard his voice below me but still couldn't look down. "Come on, Peanut, this will be OK."

I don't know if he climbed up the tree or stood way down at the bottom and guided me down, but I do remember I had the best shoulder ride back to the house, with my hands around his whiskery chin and him saying, "No more climbing in the Sunday Climbing Tree on Sundays."

Summer Sunday

Chapter Twenty-Two:

Church Sundays

Things were different the summer we were twelve. I thought Finn and I belonged with the grown-ups. We needed to go to the white church.

The Sunday specialness had little to do with religion. It meant I got to put on a dress. The summer I was twelve, I was secretly willing to exchange my faded blue shorts and T-shirt for clothes that Emma referred to as "feminine."

One sunny Sunday when we went to church, Finn and I were wearing my favorite Sunday outfit—a pale yellow cotton skirt and a white sleeveless shirt with a small collar that looked "perky" when it was turned up at the back of the neck. I loved that outfit.

Mother kept tucking and patting the collar down with a "there." I turned away and ducked and pushed it back up again.

Most of the time, my twin and I still dressed exactly alike. Sometimes we had the same clothes but in different colors. We didn't have a lot of clothes, so most choices were exactly the same. This could be a problem; we didn't always like the same things. With very few Sunday outfits, there was no guarantee that we both would be happy. This Sunday there were two yellow skirts and two white sleeveless shirts with long skinny arms protruding.

The only real physical difference between my twin and me was our hair. My brown hair was longer, pulled up in a ponytail and tied with my special, faded red ribbon. It was years later that I found out Finn and I were more different than I realized.

"I hated that skirt," she said. "It had the worst fit." By the time we were in high school, Finn was designing, sewing, and tailoring her own clothes, while I struggled to get the sleeves on the right way with an Easy Sew Simplicity pattern.

But when we were twelve, it was only the thin red ribbon around my ponytail that showed a difference.

Off we went in the blue Rambler station wagon. Dad wore his "summer suit," Mom was up front on the passenger side, and my older sister was in the back seat flanked by The Twins. She was still a big boss, her bossiness a call to arms for us; or did our twinship close her out of our partnership and force her to be bossy?

I looked at her. *Did she ever feel lonely? I never did—not with Finn near me.*

We rode up the hill of the driveway. The Sunday Climbing Tree was coming up on the right. I stared out the window at it. I focused on my reflection in the glass of the window as the tree faded to the background. I could see my face in the glass as I scornfully turned up my nose and deliberately turned away.

How could I ever have thought it was a great pirate ship?

I left behind what was really my first place of worship in nature. I traded it in for the more accepted way to worship.

The car passed like a royal coach between the double lines of rocks kept white by our whitewash brushes. Out we went onto Woodhull Landing Road and through the little town of Miller Place.

The closer we got to the Mt. Sinai Congregational Church, the straighter I sat. It made me feel more grown-up.

We parked the car in the gravelly lot and walked in through the doublewide doorway. I got satisfaction from knowing I looked pretty because a lady in the back aisle said, "Oh look, they must be twins. How cute they are." The compliment was a shared one, but I was used to that.

◆   ◆   ◆

Sitting in the red velvet pew at the Mt. Sinai Congregational Church was like waiting for a Sunday show to begin. There was so much to look at.

First, I looked back at the woman who said we were cute. She was dressed in a solid mustard-colored dress and she had stockings on! She must know about fashion. That validated her "cute" statement even more for me. I couldn't wait till I was old enough to wear stockings to church.

Next, I checked on the arriving church families, the people who lived in Mt. Sinai all year. We were not part of the church families. We were a Summer Family, going to church most summer Sundays and to the annual summer chicken barbeque. Creatures of habit, the church families sat in the same center pews each week, and so, lived in what my Finn and I called the "pew" neighborhood.

A white-haired old lady came alone each week and always sat up front—center section, first row. She was a Melancholy Spinster, oddly mixed in my mind with the picture on the *Old Maid* card deck. Odd, because she didn't look stern like the card picture. She looked soft and little, more like the tragic Miss Havisham in the musty old *Great Expectations* book I discovered on the living room shelf. I just knew a "rake" had abandoned her. Emma used that word once, and by the look on her face I knew it wasn't nice. I imagined my Sunday Miss Havisham had been left on her wedding day at that very same church and came each week, nursing a slowly dying, romantic ember.

I twisted around and looked back. Maybe the rake was in the church.

"Tell Ethel to sit still." I heard Mom start the message at her end of the aisle. By the time the order came from Mom to Ingrid, to Finn, to me, I was already gazing at the minister with fierce devotion.

But, oh, just thinking of my Miss Havisham brought a tragic sigh up and out of my small, but dramatically emotional heart. What if I were abandoned at the altar like Miss Havisham? Would I want revenge? Would I pine away like my church Miss Havisham?

I was distracted by what I called "The Boy Family" who belonged in the pew behind Miss Havisham—center section, second row, directly to the right of us. They were like a paper doll family: mother and father, both pretty boring in my opinion, and three boys, uncomfortably clothed in white, short-sleeve cotton shirts, clip-on ties, and long khaki pants. Their blond hair was always parted and slicked to the right, which gave them a look of three bland cutouts, each one slightly taller than the one at his side. Bland, yes, but *boys*, and that made me curious enough to sneak peeks at them.

My family always gravitated to the second row from the front, left section, the coveted seat being the one by the window. Dad on the outside, then Mother, then Ingrid, Eileen, and Ethel. That particular Sunday I had been fast enough to get in front so I got the window seat. The window, with white shutters pushed open, gave me a wonderful view out to the sloping hill, across the marsh to the bay and the Long Island Sound. When my mind strayed from the minister, God got my attention with the blue-green water and pale blue sky. A breeze lifted my red ponytail ribbon across my face. I pushed it back. I took in a great breath of peace and beauty.

Rising to sing *"Whaat a friend we have in Jee-sus,"* I had time for a quick look around behind me and up, up to the choir loft, that mysterious place almost more holy than the spiral staircase that led to the minister's podium. The choir seemed to have this halo—dust motes shining around them from the sunlight.

All the singers kept their chins tilted up, mouths open wide and yet kind of smiling. *How did they do that?*

Their hymnbooks rested on folded hands at their waists. It was a picture I memorized for later reenactment in front of the bathroom mirror. *"AAh-mennnn."*

"Ethel, turn around." My mother's voice.

But my dad smiled and nodded. He knew.

Amen.

Chapter Twenty-Three:

Sneakers

Near the end of school each June, we'd make our annual trip to Robert Hall, the department store for suburban families in the '50s, rivaled only by Mays. Both stores were crowded with racks of boxy, cotton clothes, and the one choice of kids for summer footwear—Keds sneakers. There were no glamorous clothes at Robert Hall. Its message was clear—good, economical clothes in all sizes. I am sure Mrs. Desmaisons' lacquered toes never stepped through the doorway of Robert Hall.

For a short while, summer sneakers were crisp white canvas, with very white laces, and plastic-covered lace tips. They were kept in their shoebox till the day of our Miller Place journey. Then, out they came to be worn six days a week for the entire summer. In about a month, my summer sneakers had no laces and several holes on the sides by my little toes from weeks of hard skipping, falling, and running on the path, the beach, and in the dusty field.

Our summer sneakers were loose and yellow gray from the sand. They were comfortable, just like the summer. In later years, I compared them to winter sneakers, which were white, tight, and had laces.

My winter sneakers were kept white with Kiwi liquid polish. If I rolled it on too late at night and they weren't dry by morning, the polish soaked through and left white blobs on my little toes. Winter sneakers were kept in my school locker during the week for gym days along with my smelly gray gym suit. A school gym suit was a one-piece uniform with an attractive shorts length. If only the shorts part hadn't blossomed out around each leg like an expanded, wrinkly balloon.

Hoping For Beauty

Girls with breasts could leave the two top snaps of their gym suit undone and get some appreciative looks from the boys' gym class as we trotted across the schoolyard for field hockey. Girls like me, without breasts, could only hope a good starched ironing, and rolling the bloomers under the elastic, would bring attention down and away from the nonexistent chest to the legs.

After gym one September afternoon, my friend Judy said, "You and your sister have such long legs. When you come back from summer vacation, you always look so nice and tan."

Wow! Someone had noticed me in a way that could fall in the "attractive" category. I looked down at my twelve-year-old legs. I had to admit that I had two pretty nice, long legs. They were almost golden tan like Starr's. Well, really more nut brown, but a smooth brown.

Maybe part of me would be beautiful.

Chapter Twenty-Four:

Dolls' Demise

"Whatever are you doing with that scarf?"

My hands kept wrapping the pink chiffon scarf around my little Ginny doll. "I'm making an evening gown for her to wear to the ball."

"But she's a little girl doll." This from my older sister who, lately, seemed to have no imagination or desire to live in fantasyland.

"No, she isn't." My earnestness in creating my idea of a grown-up world was such that physical evidence to the contrary would not deter me from experiencing the glamour of Hollywood right there on the screened-in porch in Miller Place.

It was a steady rainy day. We had played canasta for hours. Now, we had lost interest in the thousand-piece puzzle of some far away and fascinating landscape with jagged, rocky cliffs and small, colorful boats rocking in a sunset harbor. The sky was pretty much the only part left to do, and neither Ingrid nor Finn nor I wanted to sort through seven different shades of blue. Besides, it was the castle poised on top of the cliff that got me started.

My Ginny doll would live there with her Prince Charming, who looked remarkably like Cousin Hank. They would be very much in love, so there would be a great deal of hugging and kissing and giving each other love eyes. Princess Ginny would sit and read books or paint miniature pictures of her gardens while the Prince was off riding. When he returned, he would look just as handsome and dashing as when he left. He was, after all, a Prince.

His father, the King, was a Hero. Being a Hero required being strong enough to lift very heavy things and fight battles.

My dad was the ultimate Hero. My Ginny's Prince was strong, but saved his strength to sweep Princess Ginny off her feet and carry her along the garden path up to the castle. Princes were not quite ready to take on Hero qualities until they became the King. Kings needed a Queen to keep it all together. I had seen the work a Queen had to do and didn't think it was an enviable position. Better to be a Princess right now.

The oak dining table on the big porch would be a perfect castle. Finn and I laid out blocks and boxes around the thick table legs for castle furniture. I raided the little jewelry box on my mother's dresser looking for safety pins to hold Ginny's ball gown together.

Next I went to look in Mother's sewing box, which safeguarded broken rhinestone pins and bric-a-brac earrings.

◆   ◆   ◆

I remembered the spring my mother learned how to make those little round bric-a-brac circles and glue them to earring backs. She sold them at the church bazaar to make extra money. She also sold them door-to-door.

My twelve-year-old brain had figured out my mother was both shy and a snob. For a snob and a shy person to sell door-to-door was unusual—and courageous.

When either of my parents departed from the expected role, I watched carefully. See, part of me figured my mother was kind of a snob because she thought most other people were not as educated as she was. That meant their character was somehow lacking. Education was highly regarded in our house. We knew without anyone saying anything directly to us, from the time we started kindergarten, that we were expected to excel in school. And, without question, we were all going to go to college.

My dad had not finished college. Instead, he worked full time and only occasionally took courses at Hofstra University. My mother's education at Barnard College and early teaching career before she married were revered in our family history.

With all her education I don't remember seeing my mother reading for enjoyment. She had surrounded us with books since we could hold them. We had nursery rhyme books, *The Little Engine That Could*, then on to series books, *Honey Bunch*, and *The Bobbsey Twins*. I especially loved the Bobbsey Twins, wanting to be a mix of the adorable, curly-haired Flossie and the more grown-up and motherly Nan Bobbsey.

Unlike my mother, my dad read everything, from the Sunday paper to *Reader's Digest*. He also read the *World Book Encyclopedia*, starting at "Volume I Ab-Az." He would sit in the green wicker porch chair on a Saturday night. His legs were crossed so he kind of slouched to one side, and the iron ashtray stand would be at his side, smoke from his cigarette curling up into the lamplight. Once I even saw him with the big dictionary open on his lap.

"What are you looking up, Dad?"

"No word in particular. Just reading."

We read. Dad read. Mother cooked, cleaned the house, and worried about what the neighbors would think of just about anything. *Couldn't mothers ever relax?*

I also realized my mother was shy. She seemed to have only one woman friend at home who she talked to on the phone, even though they lived around the corner from each other. She talked to Nan on the black rotary dial phone just about every day. Because the phone was in the center hall, you could hear everything she said, but it was boring because all my mother seemed to say was, "Yah, mmm hmm," to Nan's side of the conversation.

At home she criticized the neighbors. "Mr. Linkley's drunk again," she'd sniff.

This was extremely odd since my own father had been brought home late at night by kind strangers for the exact same reason. He was drunk. There were murmured conversations in my parents' bedroom late at night. A plate thrown in the kitchen when dinner was waiting and waiting for the Dad who didn't come home. Although Finn and I watched his late-night, clumsy entrances into the house, no one ever said a word about it in general conversation.

The morning after such lateness, my father whistled *Sweet Georgia Brown* in the kitchen and made breakfast for us while my mother built a stony wall of silence that left us to pick a side. So I clung to my Finn.

I remember our winter house as chilly and gray. My mother mostly stayed in the house. We did not invite kids over to play.

But with the magical power of Miller Place, Dad didn't drink too much when he was there. Kids shouted and played Hide and Seek all over the property, even under the house.

In Miller Place, Mom sat with other mothers at the beach. They talked about children and the fruit on sale at Davis's Peach Farm. Miller Place is where I heard my mother laughing. She even spoke French with Mrs. Desmaisons. My mother was very educated. By family association, I figured that made me sort of smart and sort of French.

My dad may not have had a college education, but he was smart about people. No matter where my father was, he knew how to make friends.

"Hi, I'm Al Erickson," he'd say to anyone, smiling his wide smile with his hand out for a warm handshake. "This is my wife, Gladys, and my three girls," and he'd go down the line, "Ingrid, Eileen, and Ethel." All with the big smile on his face.

And we'd all follow suit. Smile and shake.

"Put out your hand. Four fingers together. Thumb up a little. Firm. Strong," he'd instruct.

I learned how to do this at a young age. I used to be embarrassed by his friend-liness; he was like that even at the grocery store. As I got older, the routine came naturally for me too, an opening that I would use beyond my childhood with new acquaintances and friendships.

Back to this business of Mom selling door-to-door. Dad worked very hard and was a "good provider," but there never seemed to be enough money to buy any extras—no extra clothes, furniture, toys, or games. We had hand-me-down every-thing. Ingrid's clothes became ours; neighborhood toys got passed around.

For Mom to do this selling on her own must have been very hard. How did she get ready to do this? Did she practice in front of her bedroom mirror? Did she do the handshake? Did she only go to people we knew because of her shyness, or did she deliberately go to people she didn't know because of her pride?

◆   ◆   ◆

My Ginny doll princess was waiting. I took four small safety pins and some remnants of purple and white bric-a-brac from the sewing box. The pins held the scarf around Ginny's pudgy body, and it draped glamorously over one shoulder. The bric-a-brac was cut to tie around her waist.

Our Ginny dolls had traveled to Miller Place since we got them when we were about six. I loved my Ginny with her yellow hair and long-lashed eyes that closed when you tilted her back. Eileen and I had been aging our dolls for several years. Ingrid was just picking up on this as she noticed the dress style and activities. This summer, the imaginary Prince who danced and put his arms around my Ginny had bestowed hand kisses and more daring physical affection.

Ingrid left for the familiarity of the blue-sky puzzle, and Ginny and I were left to enjoy the ball.

It was during our twelfth summer that doll play had the biggest change. Somehow we had played less and less with our dolls this summer. Our Miller Place world was changing. We skipped doll play to get to the beach to see who was there. We spent time watching the boys play King of the Rock, as they stole looks at us to see if we were watching.

Near the end of the summer, Honey, Eileen, and I were sitting outside on the brown flannel blanket by the swing. We were packing our dolls to go home.

"I'm packing my Ginny's dresses and scarves in this old shoe box," I said, trying not to feel guilty about such an unfashionable suitcase. "I don't think the plastic hairbrushes and bric-a-brac jewelry will even fit."

Honey led the conversation in a different direction. "Do you think we'll bring our dolls next year?"

"Well," said Finn diplomatically, "We aren't always playing here by the swing. Now we're allowed to walk up to the post office."

"And, we went up to the new candy store to buy ice cream on some afternoons," Honey said in a slow, deliberate way.

"It's been fun this summer to swim with the other kids on the beach."

The three of us knew "the other kids" meant not just Frankie, but two other boys who had joined our beach group this year.

Three wide-eyed Ginny dolls stood before us. We paused as we looked at each other without a word.

We knew what this conversation was about. Why bring the dolls when we could *be* the dolls?

"We'll probably be with the boys next year," my Finn Eileen said.

"We won't have time for dolls," Honey added.

"Is it agreed?" I asked boldly. "No dolls?"

We all nodded and finished packing.

My Ginny looked at me and slowly closed her eyes as I laid her gently in her box.

Chapter Twenty-Five:

Kissing

I was always interested in kissing.

I'd seen my father and mother kiss hundreds of times. He grabbed her and hugged her. Kisses landed on her cheek, her face, and her neck like happy butterflies finding their flowers. Sometimes he kissed her when they were dancing. Then a kiss slid from his mouth over to her cheekbone as he leaned close to her.

My great-aunts kissed me on the cheek or forehead—smiley kisses accompanied by laughs and pinches and giggles. My grandmother's sisters, Pauline, Elsie, and Ruth, reminded me of Tweedle Dum and Tweedle Dee, all short and round. They had high-pitched giggles. We knew they were glad to see us when they kissed us.

My Finn and I tried to kiss like Mrs. Desmaisons and her son, Louis. We'd try right side first, then left. We'd start sitting prim and straight with our chins tilted up and proud, but we were clumsy, bumping jaws and ended up falling over on the brown flannel blanket laughing.

I saw Hank kiss Starr right on the lips. They each tilted their faces the right way so they didn't bump; their eyes got a little crossed as their faces got closer and closer. Now *that* was the kind of kiss I was interested in. That, and the smiles that both of them had after they pulled back away from each other. They looked so relaxed and dreamy.

◆   ◆   ◆

One rainy day, Emma took my sisters and me to see the movie *An Affair to Remember*. I don't know where Mom went, but she was gone for the whole day. So Emma was minding us.

141

I felt like I had been promoted to junior high school without going through sixth grade. Mom would never have taken us to such a grown-up movie. But Emma wasn't a mother. She also wasn't really our grandmother. She was an old lady who was married to Grandpa, but she treated us like we were older, maybe like teenagers.

Because it was raining we couldn't go to the beach. In fact, Emma never went to the beach to sit with the mothers. She usually stayed in the log cabin, even on sunny days. She sang hymns, kept the cabin really polished and clean, and read *The Saturday Evening Post.*

But that rainy day we drove the ten miles to Port Jefferson to the only movie theatre around for miles to see *An Affair To Remember.* How grown-up! How cool! When Cary Grant kissed Deborah Kerr as their ship sailed under the stars at night, oh, I felt really funny inside, in a good kind of way. I saw all the happiness, pride, and dreaminess I had witnessed with teenagers and grown-ups around me in that big screen kiss.

That's when I just knew I was destined to have a great love in my life. It would probably start with a boyfriend, like with Starr and Hank, but that wouldn't be the Great One. No, that would just be a Starter, because how could I know all that Deborah Kerr seemed to know? And what teenage boy could know all that Cary Grant knew?

But somewhere there was a boy who would look at me like Hank looked at Starr, like Dad looked at Mom. And someday, someone would look at me like Cary looked at Deborah. But by then, I would be very, very grown-up.

Chapter Twenty-Six:

Sunday Cookouts

"If I eat one more bite of corn, I'll burst." Finn looked at me with a few kernels protruding from the corners of her mouth, along with the dribbles of butter that coated her chin.

My twin and I had a contest each Sunday night supper to see who could eat the most corn on the cob. Sunday cookouts were up by the fireplace, in an area past the apple trees. The old stone fireplace and wooden picnic tables were about half way up the driveway hill between our white house and the log cabin.

Ever since I could remember, anyone who lived on the property was invited to the cookout. So that meant Grandpa, Emma, Dad, Mom, Ingrid, Eileen, and me. In earlier years, it included whoever was renting the log cabin.

Having a Sunday cookout meant coming back from the beach about an hour earlier than usual to get ready. Dad opened up the shack, a barbeque stand he built on a concrete slab. There was an old sink with running water, another marvel that Dad hooked up. Jelly jar glasses lined up on white-painted shelves. Mismatched metal forks, spoons, and knives, a fireplace fork, and a spatula nested in drawers. Big potholders, thick quilted squares that were charred and burnt from close calls with the wood burning flames, hung on nail hooks on the inside walls.

The stone fireplace was a mound of rocks cemented together in Grandma Berberich's time. It was like a big stove with a grill in the center and a pit for the wood underneath. The smoke went up and out the chimney in the back. Big old maple and oak trees circled around the whole area like a high green shelter.

It took at least four trips from the house to the wooden picnic tables to set up. Finn walked up swinging a bag of paper plates and napkins. Ingrid carried trays of round, raw, chopped-chuck hamburgers, and wobbly uncooked hot dogs. Bags of corn sat by the side of the fireplace awaiting their fate in the corn pot. It was always men's work for Dad or Grandpa to tend to cooking the burgers, hot dogs, and corn. They watched the water boil until it was just right to drop in the corn that we had shucked by the garbage pit that afternoon.

An old iron handbell was up on the corner shelf by the shack door.

"Is it ready, Daddy? Is it ready?"

"Yes, yes, go ahead."

Ingrid raced to grab the bell and swing it up over her head, its ring echoing both ways up and down the drive.

"Time to eat!"

We drifted in around the wooden picnic tables, kids together, women in the middle, men at the end by the grill.

"Ooh, I love the smell of grilled hamburgers and onions!" I cupped my hands around the hamburger buns to feel the warmed hamburger buns, crispy outside, but soft and warm inside.

"Watch that ketchup bottle. It'll pour out all over you if you shake it too much," Dad said, reaching out to take it from my hands to smother his own hamburger in ketchup.

Steaming corn was stacked up in a pyramid on a chipped china platter and covered with a thin dishtowel to keep the ears warm. Mom plunked a green salad in a big wooden bowl in the middle of the table on top of the plastic red-and-white checked tablecloth, surrounded by paper plates, and heavy silver utensils.

Who wanted to eat boring green salad when there was corn on the cob! Push the butter across the corn rows, shake on lots of salt.

"Ready? Set. Go."

Eileen and I ate our corn typewriter-style, starting at the left and munching across a row of sweet Long Island yellow corn. Butter dribbled on our fingers, and the salt mixed with the melted butter on our chins.

"Ding!" I shouted when I got to the end of the row.

Then I turned the ear of corn a bit and went back to the left end for another trip across the next two rows. If I picked out an even-rowed cob, the kernels came off so smoothly.

"How many rows can you fit in your mouth without swallowing?" That was part of our contest.

Dad had an eating contest with whoever was sitting at the picnic table. Who would eat the most food? Hamburgers, hot dogs, and ears of corn? We kept a running total as we ate, reaching right across the table to grab another ear of corn, another burger, another hot dog, grinning with the success of our mealtime accomplishments.

The grown-ups' talk drifted around us.

"Good corn this week."

"Good price too."

"Girls, put these sweaters on. It's getting chilly."

"That rhubarb came from our garden."

"Pop, we'll paint that railing next weekend."

"No rush, no rush. Here, have another beer."

"Guess we'll start the cleanup soon. Eileen, stack all the utensils and glasses on the black tray. Take it into the stand. Ingrid, you go in and rinse and wash them." Mom loved to go through this drill. "Make sure those glasses get lined up on the shelves for next Sunday. Ethel, pile all the paper plates and napkins on the Rheingold tray. Then you can take it to the garbage pit."

Yes. That meant I could race to the pit to throw in the garbage.

"Daddy, I added crumpled newspaper for kindling, just enough, not too much. Can I light 'er up?"

Dad had cleverly lit the newspaper torch already and let me throw it in with his hand guiding mine.

The smell of burning garbage didn't seem awful to me. It reminded me of outdoors, family, and everybody feeling full and lazy after Sunday night cookout. The bits of burning ashes rose up towards the trees, going out just as our gazes got up to the sky.

"A shooting star. Daddy, I saw a shooting star!"

The end of another perfect weekend.

Thinking of Miller Place

Chapter Twenty-Seven:

Think of Miller Place

It was a cool autumn night. My blue wool blanket, that usually was comfort enough, could not soothe me back to sleep. My father came into the room that I shared with my Finn, Eileen, during the school year.

"Daddy, I had a bad dream."

It didn't matter what Dad said at first. "It's only a dream. It didn't really happen." That didn't work.

What lulled me back to sleep was what he said next.

"Now go back to sleep. Think of nice things. Think of swimming at the beach. Think of climbing trees. Think of Miller Place."

Think of Miller Place.

- THE END -

Epilogue

We traveled to Miller Place until my Finn and I were in high school. My last summer was 1963: the Shirelles replaced Elvis; riding in a friend's 1963 Chevy replaced pushing my doll to the ball on a wooden block; Martin Luther King's echoes of "I have a dream" replaced the Fresh Air Fund visitors.

In the summer of 1964, Finn got a job being a mother's helper. Ingrid had completed her junior year at Gettysburg College. I went to school for Driver's Ed. No Miller Place that summer.

I had a crush on the boy who sat next to me in the back seat of the 1962 Ford in Driver's Ed. The teacher, a Phys. Ed. coach earning extra money during the summer, sat in the front passenger seat focused on the trembling teenager behind the wheel. More to the point, I had an infatuation with the way my backseat classmate and I were connected. We touched knee to thigh. This was not because we were particularly attracted to each other. It was just that three kids in the back seat of the car was a pretty tight fit. I stared more at his jean-covered leg than I ever did at his face. Even on cloudy summer days, that car was hot. Hormones filled the air. I know I learned how to navigate a car in Driver's Ed. that summer, but I also learned that adolescent feelings preceded and overcame thought. So much for education, reason, and logic.

Eventually Miller Place was sold; the whole acre was split into two separate plots. My Grandfather and Emma moved to a small house in the next town, but our physical Miller Place was gone—the houses, most of the furniture, the books. Gone. My mother's pain over that loss brought tears and anger. She had always thought it would be hers—the land, the houses, the furniture, and the dishes—but it was her *mother* who had said that, not her *father*. And that made all the difference.

I was sad and disappointed, but I was still trying to operate with Ethel as center of the universe, and I didn't completely understand my mother's bitterness.

"Sold right from under my nose," she confided on the phone to Nan. I wondered what Nan's reply was. Mom only sniffed.

I knew, with a finality that protected me from hurt like Mom's, that it was Grandpa's property. He had the deed, which gave him the power to do what he wanted. He always had done what he wanted. Why would this be any different? I had thin wisps of thought of what family promises can do to shape your ambition, and what family disappointments can do to hurt you.

So I felt sad, very sad. But a larger world beckoned. New York City—I knew I wanted go to college near the city and spend time exploring museums, Broadway, and Radio City Music Hall.

I heard college friends talking about The Shore, and they meant the beaches of New Jersey.

"You mean you've never been to The Shore?" they asked.

"Well, of course I have," came my slightly defensive answer. "I spent every summer on the North Shore of Long Island in New Y—"

"No, no. The *Jersey* Shore! Come on. Manasquan, Seaside, Spring Lake. You gotta go."

Could it possibly be better than Miller Place?

Somehow, I never thought Miller Place would be ours anyway. It was my grandfather's house to do with as he needed.

When I graduated from high school, my summer boyfriend became an all year around boyfriend, but of course it didn't last. He lived in Brooklyn during the school year. Finn and I went to Wagner College—a beautiful campus on a hill with a storybook view of the New York City skyline. Our lives changed. Miller Place events were meant for summer, brilliantly sunny days, and a lifetime of comforting memories.

But the memories—no one could take them. My Miller Place sensitivities have lasted a lifetime. I see how Miller Place has influenced me more than any time or place in my life. Experiences in Miller Place built the foundation for so many choices in my life. I love being by water—the sound of it, the feel of it, the sense of calm I experience when I stand by a water's edge. Especially salt water.

A few crystal bowls, photos, and pieces of furniture stayed with our family in spite of the sale. I use the pink crystal dishes that my sisters and I so carefully cleaned for everyday use because they bring elegance to my life.

I still like to climb trees.

Walking in the woods is like going to church. I find I have photographs of tall California redwoods, wind-bent trees in Aruba, straight lines of evergreens in the snow-covered woods in Vermont, and apple trees from anywhere.

I try to explain my feelings and thoughts to friends. I feel especially drawn to being clear with younger children, so they don't feel confused. I always have a Finn to talk things over with. They may not.

The only names I call people are their given ones or humorous nicknames that they may call themselves. My twin, Eileen, is still my Finn.

I don't know where all those Miller Place people are. They were the precious people of my childhood. Memories of them have sharpened and sustained me.

My ideas of feminine beauty swirled together in memories of Mrs. Desmaisons, teenage girls (who always possess an awkward beauty by the mere fact of being young), and two-dimensional paper dolls. I never won a beauty contest, although I love singing songs, telling stories, and performing skits with my sisters. I am most happy dancing with my husband.

I have come to a place in life where most every day I am happy, joyous, and free. Ingrid and I live within a hundred miles of each other. My Finn and I are a bit closer—twenty miles. We are all married. Finn's husband's personality is like mine—a bit impulsive, talkative, the entertainer. My husband is more like Finn—somewhat serious, wise, and creative. I always say I married my twin.

We are aunts; we are great-aunts like Great-Aunt Pauline. I have a relationship with my two sisters that will probably be the longest in my life—longer than parents, husbands, friends, and professional colleagues. After all, my sisters have been here since the beginning of my time on earth. Finn and I laugh and look at each other and say, "Even before that."

My father found the power to overcome problems that made him think drinking would be a solution. My mother and father had many happy years of dancing together and seeing each of "their girls" dancing in the arms of their own husbands.

My grandparents and father have died.

My mother died at Christmas in 2006. She spoke in one-word sentences near the end of her life, but she liked to look at photos, especially the old ones of Miller Place. When I repeated the mantra, "Think of Miller Place," a small smile traveled across her face.

Think of Miller Place.

978-0-595-43877-8
0-595-43877-6

Printed in the United States
200600BV00004B/1-105/A